To my grandchildren, Samuel, Daisie, Aryanna, Emma Claire, Mia, Asher, Reece, Ryan, Carter, Amelia, Emory, Wells, and to my wife, Cindy, for her undying support.

CONTENTS

Dedication iii
Prologue... 1
Renegades of the Pines 4
The Origins 12
A Natural Sermon Prop 16
The Revival 21
"On the Wings of a Snow-White Dove"..................27
I will Take It on The Poach 42
Visitors in the Sanctuary....................................47
Robbery of the Communion Man......................... 50
Communion, Jesus and Fanta..............................55
Sweating for Jesus... 60
The Urgency of Life..63
Pass the Lemonade 68
Props and Illustrations 71
Dancing and Carousing.......................................78
I Stared at Her Shoes 81
The Day the Square went Silent 84
The Burning Cross 1960 86
The Home Visit... 89
The Wake 92
The Longevity of the Burial Process.....................96
Jesus and the Ceramic Pig.................................106
A Father's Poignant Prayer.................................109
Absalom, My Son, My son 112
The Sovereignty of God......................................117
Sweet Repose, Casket Wide Open 123
Fried Chicken, Corn Bread, and Jesus.................128
The Illustrations of Eternity 135
Schisms, Splits and Divisions.............................138
Churched and Divorced 143
Churched and College 146
Honorable Congressman Wilbur Mills 152
Exposure to Suffering 156
Hospital Protocol 163
A Case of Mistaken Identity................................167
Death, Bugs and a Fake Doctor 170
Bath Failure 174
The Double 177
The Wrong Funeral Home...................................180
Called to Pronounce 184

Saved by an Admission 186
Chicago 192
No Suds...195
Hyperthermia..198
My Dead Body 201
We Enter the Sanctum...205
Information Overload.. 209
The Drake Hotel 218
Hospital Training...233
The Language of the Sick...237
The Language of the Staff.. 241
A White Toilet Bowl...244
I Go to Mayo..247
The Unexplained 251
Appendix What?...254
Anguish..257
The Salt of the Earth..263
The Spit Collector..266
Honorable Supreme Court Justice Clarence Thomas......... 268
The Ending 271
My Little Mephibosheth 275
Acknowledgement..277
About the Author 278

PROLOGUE

This is a story about growing up in the South, sitting in a familiar pew of a little clapboard, country church, or gazing at the stained-glass windows from a bigger one in town, usually with a higher ceiling and a larger pulpit for transmission of the sermon. We came of age, in the 1960's 70's and 80's, experiencing the deep significance of the Sunday sermon, preached with evidence of the wonderful grace of God, as well as the tension of the Judgement coming. The preacher wept with both, sometimes speaking softly in one, while loudly in the other. Both were serious business. The sermons merged with culture and our upbringing to prepare us for our future lives.

We entered the assembly and heard the sermons before we were born, exposed to vibrations of sound through our mama's stomach that we cannot remember. We then entered the world and grew up watching the living testimonies of faith and failure in the lives and actions of others. We learned that there was evil and good in the world, spun around in all different manifestations. We sang joyful songs and made crafts in numerous vacation bible schools scattered throughout hot summers over many years. We gathered for baptisms in some creeks prior to the uptown baptistries that became prevalent. We attended revivals at least twice a year, Sunday-Saturday night. We sang loudly in a manner that could have damaged the structures in the neighborhood. Life was giving us involvement and treasured memories.

We were raised in homes, schoolyards, barns, fields of tobacco, corn, and peanuts, our parent's service stations or whatever enterprise they were in. Farmers regarded their parent's or grandparent's barns as something sacred to the wellbeing of the family. Births of livestock, the keeping of corn for the winter, and maintaining the tractors and plows, made the barn mandatory. If the barn burned, we knew the detrimental effects it would have on our families. Agriculture was important in those early years and was the life blood of many families as industries began to increase.

We spent Friday nights at football games under bright lights and large scoreboards. Sunday was a special day, fishing could be done after church services, behind foliage on the bank, where you couldn't be seen from the road. Generally, the day of rest did not include boating, fishing, work, or recreational activities. The television show, Bonanza, came on to late on Sunday night for respectable people to stay up and watch. It was after the Sunday evening service. Public school was early the next morning. We were all early risers. Life was caught and tamed by 6 AM.

In the mid 1960's, a four-lane highway was

constructed that split Georgia top to bottom and became Interstate 75. Our parents took us to bridges and overlooked a muddy stretch surrounded by huge road machines, as parents would exclaim, "This highway will take cars from New York to Miami." It was an incredulous thought. When completed, we could drive to Atlanta in three hours, an unbelievable time. For the last 50 years, Atlanta has always been under construction. It led one mother to say, "I'm not going back until they get it finished."

On a bright, Christmas Sunday morning in 1960, my brother and I found a metal service station with a grease rack for our model cars under the tree, unwrapped. Many times, presents were not wrapped when viewed on Christmas morning. We played for 30 minutes with the service station and then left for church services, returning at lunchtime when Christmas really began. This indicates the cultural respect and importance, during this era, for the idea, that God sent his Son, and we offered worship even on that special day.

It was a different world than today. We dealt with injustice in the only way that we could. We showed kindness and tried to change the world one deed at a time. We were wide eyed and bushy tailed. We were ready for the time that God placed us in. We were a generation to be reckoned with and we grew up ready to respond.

RENEGADES OF THE PINES

We were called "baby boomers", the demographic group that defined people born from 1946-1964, during the post-World War II baby boom. There were seventy- two million of us. We grew up expecting the world to improve. We had a solace or peace within us, something that provided an inner stability or support. It was an idea akin to a rudder on a ship or an aileron on a plane. It was a feeling that something was propping us up or preventing us from rolling sideways in our decisions. We spent a lot of time sitting in church pews with shared prayers. There was spiritual influence above us, below us, and beside us.

We were standing with our backs to an invisible support from which we could not fail or fall. We strived for some manner of what we saw as an achievement or even just a hint of greatness with a dull sheen to it. Nothing shiny. Nothing that would give us over whelming pride. We knew pride came before a collapse. We had discipline applied and loved our parents, even as children who might have lived in worse circumstances. We had a respect for those who walked nationally and ones in our family- our parents- our grandparents-even our ancestors from a distant land. We had a form of reverence for people who had walked ahead of us, we gave them grace, some did what they had to do to survive. Uniformly, they worked when they could.

Our parents wrote letters to government officials when there were problems. Our elected ones spoke at school functions and explained government by and for the people. We respected them. In seventh grade history, we learned of Hitler, Mussolini, and a host of dictators. We knew about the holocaust and the harm that some haters can do to others. In the fifth grade, we learned of the John Kennedy assassination with a phone call to the principal's office. We all knew our President, due to the Cuban Missile Crisis, a year earlier. We watched at home on a grainy, black and white television, as Kennedy revealed the missiles in Cuba and the military action, set up to prevent the entry of more missiles from Khrushchev. At school, it was called the "blockade". Bomb shelters were constructed on many properties during those years.

War with Cuba and the Soviet Union appeared eminent. We had a family meeting and my dad said, "we would go into the large vault at the elementary school, if needed." We were seven hundred miles from Cuba, not far when a nuclear missile is traveling. When the war was averted and Khrushchev backed down, President Kennedy spoke on a fuzzy, black and white television. Our parents cried and prayed. God had saved us from nuclear war by guiding our President. Now, our hero was dead.

The assassination of President Kennedy was in the middle of a school day, shortly after we had prayed for our lunch meal, the President was dead. The news spread like a galloping wildfire through the campus at recess time. We learned a new word, assassination. Many of us ran to the gymnasium to bring the news to teachers and seventh grade students at the recess exercise. One student said, "I'm glad he's dead." I wondered why he said that. Uniformly, we were sad and solemn, like something bad had happened. It was a helpless feeling, which we could not process, but we knew it was catastrophic. We drove into town a few hours later and faced a sheriff's roadblock. My dad said that was due to the killing of our President. It scarred us, like some hot poker that did not hurt in a way you could describe. It just seemed that life was different, grownups could now do bad things. There really was evil, a trait that had somehow avoided us till 1963. Our villains were shot in westerns, sprawled out and died as we watched, but we heard it was fake. My cousin said the movies used prisoners that were going to be killed anyway. He spoke with such authority that I believed him for several years.

We received this news about President Kennedy on the playground and nobody played. We all stood around, not knowing what it meant or what effect it could have on our lives. It just did not seem right to be playing and laughing. It was inconceivable to us that a grown-up would kill our President. It was an unseen cloud on our psyche that we knew life had changed and morphed into something different.

We saw Lee Harvey Oswald take a bullet and slump forward a few days later, observing from home on a black and white television screen, as he was moved from the Dallas County Jail on a Sunday morning, November 24, 1963. We watched that event after returning from church services. It replayed hundreds of times that week, showing a wounded and grimacing, grotesque face as the ammunition pierced his abdomen. Walter Cronkite, always sounding like raw gravel crunching on a southern, country road, became the bearer of bad news, announcing that Jack Ruby, a night club owner in Dallas, known well to the police, had killed him. We were tantalized and fascinated by the name, Jack Ruby. We had no Ruby's in school. We enjoyed saying the name. Jack Ruby. We repeated it all day that Monday at school.

We respected age. We studied leaders in school and marveled at how a postal worker from Kansas and later how a peanut farmer from Plains could rise to such a point as President of our country. We stood resolutely at bedside, metaphorically waving goodbye to friends and family when cancer had been untreatable at that time - our preachers and members of churches with us. We stood as children, peering like scared visitors at a zoo, through a wrinkled, clear, plastic canopy, termed an oxygen tent, completely covering the bed and its victim, a nice school teacher from the community. All burning cigarettes were left in an urn at the hospital front door to prevent a fireball of disaster. Cigarette butts were picked up as the visitors left and reused. Nothing usable was discarded.

We entered the first grade at six or seven years old. Prior to this, we had been raised by our parents at home. There was no pre-k or kindergarten in those years. We learned to read from the Dick and Jane series, sitting on our first-grade teacher's knee. Sometime in the mid-sixties, a black and white television was placed in the auditorium. Though only 32 inches, it sat on the stage upon a small table as a hundred of us sat and watched from the back of the lunchroom.

God was sent home from school in 1962 by the

Supreme Court. There was to be no organized effort by the school to allow public prayer after that date. It took a few years for the judicial tenacles to reach into the country schools in South Georgia, but it happened. Prior to that, we arose from our desks at 8:15 am, faced the front, and solemnly prayed the Lord's Prayer, straight from the King James Version. Our teachers led the prayer as they stood beside their desks, all of us standing beside our own.

"Our Father who art In Heaven, hallowed be thy name, thy kingdom come, thy will be done, on earth as it is in heaven, give us this day, our daily bread, forgive us our trespasses as we forgive those who trespass against us, lead us not into temptation, but deliver us from evil, for thine is the kingdom, the power, the glory, forever and ever, Amen". We liked to say "trespass against us" as its meaning was unknown, but sounded like we could have been mistreated.

We had already stood at 8 AM and pronounced the Pledge of Allegiance to the flag hanging at the front of the room, our hands solemnly across our hearts. We then sat and learned reading, writing and arithmetic, sometimes at the hands of old maid schoolteachers, of which we were deathly afraid. A least one student a week stood beside a desk and received one lick with a paddle. Another lick was given at home when the news arrived.

We stood at lunch, again solemnly, and recited our gratitude for the food. "God is great, God is good, let us thank him for our food, by his hands we are fed, we thank God for daily bread." It was a repetitive mantra, but it sealed in our hearts our thankfulness for God and his care. We then ate what was in the lunchroom without complaints.

We loved our schools, we loved our libraries, with portraits of the founders of our country including scientists like Jonas Salk and Louis Pasteur. There were yellowed bottles high on shelves with babies in various stages of development for our perusal. We took tests and tried to achieve as our parents encouraged and prodded us on. We ran through the playground like a pack of hyenas, throwing rocks and slipping on the bars and pedals of our engineered recess.

A perfect spherical red-hot candy would choke the pupil standing beside the desk, until the teacher slapped between her shoulder blades sending it 30 feet across the room bouncing off the blackboard. The shaken student resumed her studies with an ashen face. All in the day's work of a teacher. As we left for recess, we walked by the flagpole with flag flapping loudly above us, recalling the black and white television shows we saw at home, with soldiers saluting a flag on deck of an aircraft carrier as flags flapped above. Our feet invariably took pace with the sound of the flag as we marched into the playground.

Our report cards were serious business. We had a heading called "deportment" which we could not spell, but knew it was our behavior. We behaved. We also knew to return the report card with an authentic parental signature. There were no thoughts of a forgery. Why invite severe disciplinary measures? Report card day was serious.

Our teachers were dedicated and proficient. The seventh-grade teacher promised to "stand on his head" if a certain known flunker would make an A on the next test. We studied with the reprobate daily for a week, pounding the material into his head. He made an A. The teacher needed help to fulfill his vow. Lying on his desk prone, he asked us to slide him out and lower him on his head, slowly. It was a memorable, exciting event, and none of us have ever forgotten it. It was the involvement of a teacher with his class.

Growing up, we knew God was with us. We knew, like we knew the sun was coming up, hung in the sky like a fireball over the South, baking the landscape. We knew God was there, in our homes, in our cars, in our school bus. There was a known presence, and it did change some behavior. This belief held us together, it was a metamorphosis of God, guts, glory, family, and pine trees; football and baseball were in the mix.

We had scads of tall, skinny, and thick pines. They were like old friends. They surrounded our schools, surrounded our home, loblolly, and other strange names. Magnolias trees were planted by the wealthy. They lined driveways in homes most of us would never see within. They required a rake boy to remove hundreds of heavy leaves. Touching a white magnolia bulb would result in a brown stain within 24 hours right on the blossom on the tree. Owners did not want a hand to reach upward to touch a bulb as you raked. Magnolias allowed the drinking of mint julips or water under tortuous limb structures like deformed appendages and arms, as they hung over porches and roofs. They provided shade for the wealthy. In the country a shotgun house was a castle if a magnolia graced the front yard and shielded one side of the porch swing from the sun. Skeletal like roots were visible on the ground underneath the tree.

There was one beside my grandmother's house, close enough that the leaves had to be raked. The warning was always spoken, "Don't reach up and touch the bulbs."

The pines were for the masses. They were planted by the thousands, but some were called volunteers by their ability to take over a farm, if not burned and removed every year. Heavy winds could uproot them easier than the magnolia, due to shallow root systems. Some fell, we then ran along their trunks, giddy at having conquered such a monster. Pine straw drifted to the ground and was raked up for the flowerbeds. To the dismay of parents, we stuck our fingers into the small troughs hanging on the sides of the trees holding the draining sap. Turpentine could cure all ills. We smeared it on our friends. The resin stuck to our body and our clothes, but we loved to do it. It was collected periodically by dark skinned men in faded denim and poured into buckets and drums, for all manner of health benefit.

We were renegades of the pines spending time in the woods, climbing magnolias, running amuck through wet yards and barefooted in chicken houses, the chicken droppings squished between our toes, held under the spicket for removal.

There was plowed dirt, fixed between our toes, giving us the pleasure of living on dirt roads. Merging with it, we became one with the soil. We embodied the dirt and loved it. We smelled the sweet smell of tobacco cooking in the barns all night, our fathers and grandfathers checking the temperature gauge on the side of the tobacco barn at midnight. The sweet smell of cooked tobacco wafting across the dirt yards while cows raised their noses at midnight to catch the smell. God was by our side, with visons of a better life in our heads. The future was splashed before us, to seize, conquer and rule. It waited patiently, for our arrival.

THE ORIGINS

S weat hugs the body like a living organism, crawling along the skin, then rolling to a stop at the nearest boundary, be it collar, seam, or belt. It is the South, primarily in the summer. We were all used to it and thrived in it. Air conditioning was for some faraway big city in the northern distance. The dirt roads of the South did not carry air conditioning units until the late sixties. The automobiles got it first. Sometimes it was cheaper to buy a car without it and pay Sears Roebuck to install one, a black plastic box on the hump with a couple of vents, which could be described as a feeble draft. Even in a car, 460 air conditioning was the norm- 4 windows down, 60 miles an hour.

The South and summer were the perfect combination and a petri dish for the fire and brimstone sermon. Its origination over centuries in the ninety-degree heat was a natural phenomenon. You could feel Hell and the unforgiveness of your own soul while sitting on a hard pine church pew surrounded by like-minded believers.

The first row of pews was usually scarcely inhabited while it awaited the ones that would come forward in that song of invitation or altar call. When the preacher stepped into the pulpit, the train left the station. You were aboard or left lying on the trestle. The sermon advanced, rise and fall, crescendo and valley, all expressed with scripture and commentary. The door to Hell was opening wide for admittance of the unrepenting souls. Do you want to change your eternal address, from a post office box in Hell to a wonderful eternal life at the shore of Heaven? The time is now, today is the day of salvation.

The invitation was extended as the voice softened and recounted, "the lesson is now yours, friends." The forgiven would march to the front row, grown men with fresh, salty tears on their cheeks, sometimes accompanied by wives or children, making confessions and between confessions and praying with the minister. The movement to the front row, the mourner's bench or the altar was as natural as apple pie and baseball in 1960. No one was ashamed to make that walk, sometimes in a tent revival, sometimes in a clapboard church building, or down the wide aisles of the city churches.

Peter in Acts 2 had a similar oratory led by the Holy Spirit. He pointed at the large crowd and said, with his own confession, "we're not drunk as its only 9 AM", an odd admittance, for sure. He gave a history of the risen Jesus, though David their patriarch lay graveyard dead in his tomb around the corner, lying there for many centuries. He did not recount fire and brimstone, but the implications were clear. He charged them, in a forceful voice, "you have crucified the son of God." The crowd was told what they had done. They were penitent. They screamed the question, "What should we do?" That was all it took, 3000 hit the aisle, or plain or mountain and repented, confessing Jesus as the son of God. Lining up for baptisms, the church had remarkable growth, despite persecution, only days after the crucifixion of Jesus.

This was the first sermon recorded after the death and resurrection of Jesus, though the prophets had preached judgment hundreds of years before. There is no doubt in the New Testament that Jesus believed in and warned about the reality of Hell. He describes it in detail in Matthew, Mark, and Luke. When Paul wrote Romans, he admonished the reader, "how shall they hear without a preacher?" (Romans 10:14)

The message was handed to the apostles over a three-year period of training. They were then sent into the world at the ascension of Jesus, his last admonition involved movement, Go. Stephen, the deacon, delivered a similar sermon, as Peter, in Act 7, but it was not received in that earlier manner. This time, the audience was enraged, rather than hit the aisle, they hit and stoned him. This is the only instance recorded, metaphorically, of Jesus arising and standing by his throne, while observing Stephen's stoning and death. Stephen, as he died, said, "I see the son of God standing by the throne." What a beautiful way to end life on earth with a vision from above. At that moment, Stephen knew that he had done the right thing. Faith solidified, justified, soon to be glorified.

So, what is the outcome of the American pulpit. In some years, did we overlook justice and peace and focus on judgement? Did we hear a vendetta or the gospel? In the 19th century, Dwight Moody said that the judgement sermon informs us that "the Lord is coming again" and talk of hell takes the "men of this world out of stocks and bonds." Good analysis.

Jonathan Edwards, Charles Finney and George Whitefield, and others, preached fire and brimstone, as well as the grace of God, but received more fame for their fiery sermons.

Paul makes it clear that the believer has hope. A message of Jesus guiding the saved through life and God's grace upon us is of paramount importance and should tamp down the delight that the congregation might perceive in a speaker taking pleasure in sending one down a burning thread to soak in a fire.

Nevertheless, a condemnation or denunciation of bad behavior from the pulpit seems to rake like nails on a chalk board to ears of the 21st century. It is pleasurable to be at ease in Zion, with a worldly satisfaction and contentment. However, sermons are a part of our national spiritual conscience and our history in this nation. We heard it often and we thrived. We also listened, as ministers expounded on the grace of God and his love for mankind. Blessed redemption. Praise be to God. To those of us blessed to hear these sermons, it remains a part of us today.

A NATURAL SERMON PROP

He entered the pulpit in 1966 with the appropriate attire, a dark suit, starched, tight fitting white shirt, exaggerating the bony frame, an oddity for a revival preacher. Usually, a traveling evangelist was a bit heavier from the caloric consumption that was required on a weekly basis. Skinny preachers were rare in the general population of preachers. His eyes bulged slightly, was it thyroid issues or the strangulated tie pressing on the carotids? He had on cufflinks, not a common part of the usual attire, silver, slightly visible at the sleeve, no gold, as this would be considered a bit flamboyant for a man of God.

The building was called "clapboard." a white structure built in the 1930's. There was no air-conditioning, and the bathroom- the outhouse, was behind the church. A window box fan was blowing sideways across the audience, there was no ventilation in the pulpit. Thoughts of comfort for the preacher were sparse. He was on his own. The air had heated up quickly around the 150 people assembled as they sung the "Old Rugged Cross." The preacher would never remove his coat, regardless of the temperature.

The preacher began perspiring quickly as he began the sermon, first visible on his forehead. It bubbled up and ran down around the bulging eyes. He had an unusual attribute, almost a prop for the sermon, a burn scar on his entire cheek involving part of his ear. A burn has no sweat glands and the adjacent glands on the body sweat profusely to accommodate. The etiology of the injury was unknown. Preachers would generally make a comment on some obvious disability or trait. One evangelist had lost his arm in an agricultural accident as a child and duly told of the event.

The burn was appropriate because the sermon was on hellfire with brimstone added for good measure. The prominence and visibility of the deformity made some in the congregation uncomfortable. They squirmed initially as the sermon progressed, unable to avoid looking at the results of fire on a human face. The implication was obvious.

In the introduction, the preacher admonished that Jesus talked more about hell than he did heaven but he was speaking most of those times to the religious leaders of the day, who were wearing their robes and pieces of cloth with scriptures tacked on their foreheads. They had the outward signs of religion. They wanted all to know of their perfect state. They were Pharisees and they were not fair, you see. They rejected the Christ of the Cross.

They blamed Jesus for associating with the dirty people, the unchurched, the tax collectors. the prostitutes, who came with interest to see this man who was the Son of God. He told the woman at the well that he was the Messiah.

The preacher screamed, "Could we be legalists today?" The group was taken aback, they had never heard this line of thought. It was an afront to their reputations. He continued, "With our shined shoes, our hair plastered to our heads, our suits, our ties, our Bibles prominently displayed and pounded? His head turned sideways, with emphasis, and it was noted that the lower lobe of the ear on the burn was missing.

"Do we consider ourselves better, since we are here and they are not?" as he pointed at an empty pew. "Well, yes, it is better to be here, but not at the expense of judgmental attitudes, dismissing those we think are not worthy of a church pew." He screamed, "The pious are in the pews today, or are they?"

He turned to a blackboard behind him on the podium, taking a piece of chalk, and drew two columns, one labeled the saved and one branded as lost. He faced the audience, and asked, where is your name tonight? Is it in the lamb's book of life or in that column labeled "lost". God can add it to either column.

The he burst forth, the calm voice gone, it became direct, loud, and a few decibels higher. "Hell waits for those who are prideful, boastful, judgmental, stingy, miserly, unhappy souls who await a friend's demise, thieves and stealing money from the deceased." He quoted Paul, "their god is their belly." A baby cried and was carried to the nursery. The sermon was now in full swing, the train had left the station, the babies were disturbed. When the babies cried, the sermon was at the fifty-yard line. It was marching down the field, goal posts were in sight, so was lunch.

He removed from his pocket, a large two-inch ball bearing, likely from a machine of some sort. He held it high and said, "Imagine that the earth is made of this material and is a ball the size of the earth", "an ant walks around the circumference of the earth, and when the earth is worn down to this size," he holds up another marble sized ball, much smaller, then he says, "eternity will have just begun." He pauses for that to sink in and says, "Glory."

He borrows a line from Jonathan Edwards and says, "sinners are held above hell by a thread, and friends, the thread is on fire." "Suspended over eternal loss." The word "fire" was screamed at an octave higher than the rest of the sermon. Another baby cried. Unless one listened closely, "fire "sounded like "far."

Older children squirmed in the lesson prompting the speaker to separate two of his children, mid sermon. This was done publicly by reprimanding and asking the two to sit on different pews. Chastised in public was not common, but certainly was not rare. It was a public scolding of which more would be discussed at the noon meal. One preacher would motion for the talking teenagers on the back row, to please come down and sit "here" as he pointed to the front pew.

The word "rambunctious" was used frequently in those years, both in sermons and in private. Nobody could spell it, unless he was above thirty years of age. Most could not pronounce it. But it was thrown around in disciplines both public and private. "Do not be so rambunctious. "The father would loudly declare. The children had no idea what it meant, but it sounded complicated and sinful and that was all that mattered.

The sermon wound down with an invitation to line the front row with the penitent, the bereaved and the lost. Several responded. Prayers were made, response cards were filled out. A few requested a visit from the preacher, most did not. The service ended.

The children ran out past the preacher at the back door, taking a glance sideways at the burn for a closer look. "That's scary" one was heard to say.

Another, paused and said "you're crazy." An adult, hearing this criticism, immediately advised the preacher, "Don't pay attention to him, he just repeats what he has heard." The preacher's eyes widened, but he did not make a comment.

The children scattered in the church yard. If a night service they were running through the lights from the cars and searching for frogs to catch. A delinquent child would grab a frog and amaze his friends with feeding the frog Daisy BBs from his pocket. The tongue of the toad would fly out like a strand of spaghetti and catch the BB which disappeared with the tongue. The toad then would hop out, full of metal. Children were caught, packed up with their families and the church yard went silent.

It was the aftermath of the fire and brimstone sermon. Bedtime was close, time was advancing, eternity was closer than it had been the day before. A tired preacher goes to bed late that night. He paused to wonder, as sleep overtook him. Did the sinners repent or even relent? Were the baptized converted, or just getting wet? Were attitudes and hearts changed? He admitted that he would never know, in this life, nor was he expected to. That was God's business.

THE REVIVAL

It was a sultry, hot southern summer night, the kind that sticks to you with its own identity. Sweating profusely, the preacher was in a suit and strangulated tie, the standard uniform for sermons in 1960. There were no starched jeans in the pulpit yet, no shirts hanging to the midsection. No loafers with naked feet inside of them. Denim had not yet made its entrance. Midway through the sermon, the cadence and rhythm were obvious, apparent and loud. The voice was an artform, syllables rising and falling with salient points and features of their own. Behind the podium, the doors at the front of the church were open, as if to say to say, "God, bless us with moving air".

Conviction of sin hung like vaporized sweat, the elephant in the room. All of the congregation sweated and perspired like the preacher. The pews were hard because salvation was not an easy challenge. Padded pews were avoided in those years as this would leave the sinner at ease in Zion, unsaved and to comfortable.

It was revival time in Tennessee. The preacher had traveled from Georgia as he did yearly at the same church, close to his childhood home. It was in the deep country, far removed from town, 70 miles from Nashville down Highway 100. The sound of constant crunching of the gravel roads filled the building as the souls arrived. Gravel became still, the church was full and the singing began. It was loud and involved. Small children held songbooks for their grandmothers. The congregation stood with the song just prior to the sermon, a little exercise before solemn acceptance.

The preacher had waited patiently, singing loudly and valiantly on the front row. He had been privy to a huge meal of southern cooking prior to the service. Somehow, probably from gastrointestinal experience, he was able to bellow out "Sweet Hour of Prayer" without missing a note. Meals were voluminous at revivals and members and invited ministers never disappointed the cooks. That would have been a sacrilege, not to partake of the fellowship of a family. The preacher was invited before each nightly service for a meal. There, between ample helpings of fried chicken and potato salad, the fried and non -fried food groups sparkled in their pans. The non- fried were the turnips, okra, greens, peas, pear salad and a host of refrigerated dishes. The preacher would hear the stories of the congregation that occurred since his last visit, some backsliders again mired in the mud of the hog pen. They were caught having sampled a bottle of moonshine and fallen in the mud, found by neighbors and revived- for the revival- now standing on the front row, singing loudly, "Revive us again." The song was sung so often and with such force, it seemed the roof could blow off from the decibels and disappear into the heavens.

Once, a preacher chose gluttony for one of the sermons, he vowed with his magnanimous frame that he would not participate in such revivalist sinful behavior. Gluttony. He pronounced that he would not eat like a hog. Members told, that when he ate with them, he ate handily.

Always, the mainstay of the fellowship table was fried chicken anchored in line with potato salad. Gallons of sweet tea were used- banana pudding by the bucket. Greens of every variety. Hoe Cakes, with usually two meats, and always deviled eggs graced the table. Parents were adept at having their children get extra eggs for the parents. One lady was incensed with giving the devil a praise, and called them "angel eggs." They were so common that I wondered if it had something to do with keeping the devil out of the revival by the mentioning and eating of the angel eggs, keeping his name away from our conscience.

Revivals were seven days straight. White building, clap board. No brick. Pine pews. No Christianity lite or shortened sermons. A revival was nine sermons. Seven days. Attendance was stable at every service. The children were expected to sit and be still. If a child moved, he was "wiggling like a worm in hot ashes." If someone missed, a visit was generally made, inquiries advanced. This was not so much chastisement but concern. Church was a family; a group takes care of its own-whether you deserved it or not.

One member was articulate in excuses for missing the Sunday services. She would drone on in these home visits by the preacher as to her unhealthy body. She could travel from organ to organ with description of ailments such that one preacher labeled it an "organ recital." She had the maladies down and when she finished, you didn't want what she had and suddenly her quarantine seemed plausible.

In 1960, we knew God was with us. We were taught at home, in school and at every event. An athletic event was a time for prayer. God was welcomed on the field with the players. Just as the sun rose in the sky every day, we knew God was our protector and our shield. The moon, stars, the sun, the love among us and even the fried chicken on the table attested to the fact. God was real. He was as real as our mama and our daddy. We believed it then; we believe it now.

The ground at the cross was level. No one towered above another. Pride was checked at the foot of the cross. The soldiers brutally and forcefully extended Jesus' nail punctured hands on the cross, inadvertently showing the world that Jesus invites us, even in a torturous act of man's design, to come to him.

The sermon progressed but it was a wise preacher who realized when his time was up. If he detected wearied worshippers, with eyelids sagging, the invitation was quickly extended. Several verses sung loudly echoing off the hills in the valley. A visibly shaken sinner went to the front row. The sinner walk was traversed usually in the hymn, "Just as I Am", several verses resonated, one after the other. The confession was taken with the man standing before the crowd. "Yes, he believed Jesus was the Son of God." He was a shy farmer, not used to being on display, but he faced the crowd and admitted his faith. Prayers were uttered, church adjourned. Like Philip and the eunuch, he wanted baptism right then. There was no baptistry.

Regular clothes were used, baptistry garments were rarely available in country churches. It was considered an unnecessary expense. It was the courtly congregations of the city churches who expected to see the baptismal candidate in a white robe as he walked down the baptistry steps. The preacher in the city churches used his own rubber waders, he was submerged from the waist down, while the candidate was duly dunked. Multiple hanging garments were in their baptistry closet.

These buildings of the town were brick and some had stained glass, a real luxury inside the city limits. It seemed to mellow the sin with stained glass and huge oak doors, the sinner can't be too bad in a choir robe or standing under such an immaculate building, stained glass and sunlight reflected off his penitent demeanor.

Someone said, "let's take him to 'Sanken". Another said, "Sanken" has moccasins". Sanken was Sinking Creek in the dialect. As children played in front of the bands of car lights in the grass at the front of the building, they heard this interchange. They stopped and ran to the mildly heated discussion. One farmer was adamant. There was clear and present danger. The place was loaded with snakes on the bank. "Wait till morning." he said. "This could be dangerous."

The preacher said, "let's go, he wants it now." It was all the encouragement the spirit filled crowd needed. They were ready for movement. Mobility desired on a hot summer night. Mission accepted. Cars flew out of the driveway of the church and headed down the road. A salvation caravan inching along graveled pathways. The crunching sound was reverberated again. Turning down a slope, multiple headlights fanned out and shone on the water. Reflections bounced shapes around like fearful goblins from the trees onto the water. It was running swift. The children shuttered and waited for a hideous scream of pain. A flashlight searched for snake heads visible above the water. One man thought he saw one duck into the mire, disappearing below ripples of water. Where was the old dog back home who would dive in, catch one, and sling him sideways till the snake was like a limp discarded dishrag? A hasty entrance was made into swirling water. The water was too cold for verbose prayers uttered by the preacher and his party. Prayers were brief, the submerging was quick. Same clothes from the revival, minus the coat and rarely shoes. Down, down went the man's body and then rising from frigid water for a needed breath of air and the goal of a clear conscience according to Peter a few thousand years ago.

God spared his followers the snakes and the water seemed to warm. Finally, the service was over, until tomorrow night.

"ON THE WINGS OF A SNOW-WHITE DOVE"

Ferlin Huskey crooned from the top of the old white Frigidaire in 1963. A radio, AM only, screamed loudly, as it sat high so the children could not touch it. A white-haired petit woman rambling with pots and pans was making lunch. She moved from stove to sink as a single burst of steam came from the boiling pot. Music filled the room, "On the wings of a snow-white dove, he sends his pure sweet love, a sign from above, on the wings of a dove. "The petit woman sang along, her apron moving with sound and energy of its own, as the music ricocheted off the pine walls of the kitchen, battering the air like waves from a beach, bottled up, captured and let go. It was as if the sound was released on its own recognizance, to determine its own fate, to fade away followed by the next verse. This was amazing to a ten-year-old in 1963. How could a box with a dim light be responsible for creating the image of a dove floating in the kitchen above the okra? There was this picture in the mind of a snow-white dove following and dancing behind my grandmother around the room. The merger of life mixed and mingled with God, right there in a kitchen in 1963 in rural Georgia. It was not unusual and was repeated all over the South.

The grandmother could tell a story. She was born in 1895, raised after her mother's death by an aunt, who told the story of being present as a child when Sherman and soldiers came through Central Georgia in 1864. He spared the farm buildings if the family would cook him supper. As the meal was prepared, the men stood in front of the fireplace warming in the cold. When they sat down, they uniformly had to jump up due to burning from the uniforms on the backs of the legs. This caused laughter among the children. The soldiers were nice and caused no problems, leaving after the meal.

Grandparents in those days were aware of the power of evil and the mayhem with man that it can cause. It was not unusual to hear a grandparent say, "Get behind me Satan.", in an effort to thwart whatever bad thoughts were out there.

We were almost universally close to God, attendance at the church services was the metric. Most all of us attended church three times a week, maybe four if you counted Sunday School. Commerce was slowed early on Wednesdays to allow time for attendance at the weekly prayer meeting. There were a lot of churches. If you missed, you generally received a visit. The ones in the pews could name the ones not in the pews. The absentee list was watched closely. Two weeks absence was serious. In those days, preachers, like doctors, made house calls. The party was asked, "what's wrong with you?"

The popular Baptists were on every corner, all

flavors and brands. Leanings were modern or primitive. Most churches in town had relatively new brick buildings, unlike the clapboard of the rural areas. Contribution and tithing were heavier in the prosperous churches within the city limits. It was reflected in stained glass windows and missionaries to the Congo. Occasionally, a church sign said, "authorized King James Version." A paraphrased edition was nowhere near a printing press yet, neither was the New International Version.

There was a good supply of the Pentecostal variety, with signs of the Holy Spirit amply manifested. The Church of Christ sang loudly and studied music at 5:30 PM on Sundays. By age ten, boys led singing and could scream an octave or whisper a verse. There were the quiet Nazarenes, a smattering of Catholics, and Methodists had a large number. There were the educated and prominent town Presbyterians, who some referred to as the "frozen chosen", by their own admission. A Jewish delegation completed the mix. Seventh Day Adventists could serve fake bacon that tasted delicious. Mormon friends used no nicotine, alcohol or caffeine. All of us were friends and knew that God was watching us.

Primarily, churches had a piano and not the general use of multiple high-volume instruments in the worship service. Fog and smoke machines were rarely in bars, certainly not in churches. Padded pews were still a controversial topic, many felt that sin was made comfortable while graced into a quilted pew.

Music in 1960, in a general sense, was not a dominant force in society as it is today. The Statler Brothers and Naomi, The Ordinaires, Elvis with "How Great Thou Art" were commonly heard on the radio. The Beatles came across the pond and hit America with a storm. Gyrating and moving brought changes to the music in both church and society. It was eventually a powerful a sea change. The sixth-grade teacher said, "the Beatles were popular for one reason, they were louder than any other group." "It was the sound banging on our eardrums that would make us gyrate and move uncontrollably." It sounded scientific and we wanted to agree with her, but we couldn't, we all wanted Beatle boots, the records, a Beatle haircut, and a trip to the Atlanta Stadium to see the show August 18, 1965. The Atlanta Journal advised us how to get a Beetle haircut. It was 30,000 fans that heard the show. I heard the ruckus from the road as we drove by, that was as close as I got. I was 12 years old and no way were my parents taking me into that stadium.

Music gradually merged into becoming a basic part of life, not just an activity that you bought tickets for and sat and listened. It became a dominant force in Christian culture.

We all belonged to church youth groups, meeting at times and learning scriptures. We could recite the 66 books of the Bible quite easily by age 6. A big summer event was Vacation Bible School which placed us all in front of flannel boards, lemonade and crafts. Beads in mass were used to form Bible verses. Bottles of Elmer's glue were used by the case. Construction paper was standard tan unless multicolored sheets could be obtained.

Church services were attended, sometimes, the less excited members on the back row, with the staid and solemn on the front rows, glancing intermittently to determine who was present or more importantly, who was absent. Both groups of Christians were known to the other. Reasons for absence quickly passed across the minds of those in attendance. Disinterest, boating, fishing, dancing, liquor or moonshine hangovers were possibilities. Late night activities were envisioned that could make a person sleep late on Sunday, attending the church aptly named, "Mattress Springs". The preacher might say from the pulpit, "there are those who have not darkened the door of this church in months." I visualized the shadow of a big man passing across the clean white facing of the front door as the preacher espoused the congregation on the virtues of attendance. "Forsake not the assembly" was spoken appropriately and with great vigor.

We maintained "Sunday shoes" shined on Saturday night. They were not worn at other times except funerals and weddings. Their home was the closet floor, below the suit, which was not worn except on Sunday. We wore ties and white shirts. Our hair was meticulously combed and plastered to the scalp with Vitalis, a yellow mixture with consistency of medicinal liniment, which would make a cow lick lie down on the back of the head as flat as a pancake. A thick, wild, mop of hair on a squirming 10-year-old could be tamed in 2 minutes with a massage of Vitalis and a large comb pulled from the cupboard in the kitchen. The hair laid down as it was scraped to the scalp in some manner between torture and what was called "getting ready for church". A final inspection was given by the father or the mother at the front door prior to leaving the porch and entering the car. At that point, faces were wiped again, absent belts were found and children were sent to brush their teeth. The inspection was mainstay every Sunday before the door was opened.

The Pentecostals and Church of God had the louder and more energetic services than the quiet liturgical fare of some. Grown men screamed and raised hands, children followed and infants cried. Glossolalia, the speaking in tongues was performed. Some Christians called it "babble" but the holy rollers were not dismayed. Large crowds gathered, some with curiosity, others not wanting to miss being "slain in the spirit". It was quite contagious and catching for the crowd and could motivate the disinterested to a new level of involvement. The Holy Spirit cannot be underestimated, regardless of our criticism.

A young visiting child later asked her mama what it meant for "a preacher to get out of hand," as overheard from a relative. Her mother responded by asking what behavior the preacher had exhibited, "anything unusual?" The child said "yes, a chair was broken, one leg." TThe mother then understood, but the child went away unsure.

Every town had a periodic tent revival filled with loud sermons and multiple collection baskets as the love offerings ran up and down the pew passing the metal chairs like a binding chain. Crickets were heard seeming to chirp in unison and with the cadence of the speaker. Both crickets and preacher were loud. The affair could last 2 weeks and usually had familiar speakers who were seen yearly in such gatherings. The metal chairs sat lop sided because they were placed on grass, freshly cut, or sometimes on a canvas tarp like floor. The chairs could be unstable for the larger Christians and occasionally a chair would sink awkwardly, tilt, and dump the listener into the floor. The unstable would scramble to right up the chair and resume the seating as if nothing had happened.

The tents overhead usually had a drip when the rains came during the service. It was impossible not to have a drip in a South Georgia gulley washer of a rainstorm. Chairs were slid away from the water entry above, and created zig zagged seating through the audience. Water dripped quietly from God's heaven through the canvas tent as the preacher expounded.

The children did not want their chairs moved, as they wanted the drip on their heads for entertainment. Babies tolerated all they could and intermittently cried from fatigue in these lengthy services. The seasoned preacher would say, "that is the most wonderful sound on earth", spoken with a booming voice above that of the screaming child. Afterall, what could he say? Nothing he said could make the baby relent. Silently, he prayed that the Holy Spirit would temporarily paralyze the vocal cords. However, the public mention made the mothers beam with pride and reddened faces, as Junior screamed, as if held against his will awaiting a death sentence.

One volatile, charismatic speaker became so incensed over a band of babies disrupting and crying at an important sermon point that he lost his composure and piped loudly that nobody, including the children, would listen or repent, accusing the group of being "bowed up in the back", a metaphor for the strong willed unrepentant, hell bound. He stomped out down the aisle through the back door, never to preach there again.

Crying and disruptive children was not an uncommon event, it was, of course, predictable, with adults struggling to decipher a sermon with a lot of lengthy illustrations and sub headings. This happened 2000 years ago at a similar gathering. Jesus rebuked his disciples when they became incensed over youthful behavior. He shut them down, advising them that, "you must become as little children to enter the kingdom of heaven." They must have scratched their heads on that one. You could say that's a pretty good recommendation of Christianity, from the Son of God, to behave as little children, loving and forgiving, yet prone to tantrums. Our behavior is not the entire breaking point of the Christian life, because Jesus knows exactly what our behavior will be, since we are human after all. He provides grace, forgiveness and instruction from his Word. I bet the disciples sequestered and mumbled on about that admonition. A radical idea like that today could split a church.

Hence, enter Children's Church, a location born for the disruptive and others who would do anything to be removed and absent from the worship service, even as a volunteer. This took root by the 1970's which involved separation of the children from the pious in the sanctuary. The idea was not bad, it could be a place of training, a place of learning, a place to get used to sitting still and not squirming like Tom Sawyer under the watchful eye of the Widow Douglas. It had some controversy, as some parents felt it was their responsibility to train their own children how to behave, not the church volunteers. The idea of having a separate group from the adults was met with varied opposition. As with most church debates, it became quite spirited.

The idea seemed to function better in the stained glass, brick and mortar churches of larger towns than the country clapboard building where the babies were crying and the adults seemingly tolerated it better, accustomed to such disruptions. One member recounted that the problem was lengthy sermons, to which nobody including an infant could avoid being restless, when subjected. He related, that if preachers were reduced to the more scriptural 20-25 minutes, most of the crises would be eliminated, hence, no need for children's church and separation. A member wondered if there was truth to that.

A preacher or two did heed the warning of reducing his word output on Sunday morning. It resulted in two victories. One was allowing the flock to beat the plentiful Baptists to the downtown cafeteria for the wonderful Sunday meal. The other was the evaporation of the controversy which threatened the unity of the body, and the children stayed comfortably with their bottles and coloring books in the auditorium.

One child, jerked up and taken out, was admonished by the red-faced parent, "I think the devil has a hold on you!" the child replying loudly to the congregation, "I think he does too!"

Other large churches went full throttle, children escorted from the auditorium in a marching celebration to a location where sound would not travel, instituting a full service geared to the youth without the watchful eye of parents and limited crying. This worked out well and laid ground work for a host of other ministries and committees which always seem to thrive in organized worship. This led to puppet groups, musical intervention, various snacks, all in an effort to keep the parents calm and collected back in the auditorium, able to receive God's grace in peace. No family was forced to part with their children and indeed, some children continued to sit in the sanctuary, learning behavior from parental guidance. As always, there were many opinions where church matters were concerned.

Parents were uniformly against dancing, drinking, and mixed bathing, as it was called. These were the three major sins of the 50's and 60's. These could be subdivided into a flow chart, perp algorithms but these were the bigger headings. Sermons sometimes seemed to hover for weeks around one of these sins with great emphasis and oratory.

The fact that David danced with limited clothing and Paul recommended a "little wine for stomach's sake" were not mentioned in these tirades of morality to squirming members on hard pews on Sunday mornings, some bleary after a shot or two of whiskey on Saturday night. Better to come and face the music than lay out and have half the church appearing at your farm during the week with, "What's wrong with you?", "Anything I can do?" "We are here because you are of the household of faith."

Sitting wide eyed with broken capillaries, visible was at least present and accounted for, and would tamp down any visitations at the corn crib by the preacher and his entourage the following week. The invisible word was "accountability" and this was the unspoken thought. We were all accountable for our behavior in those times, and it might be mentioned at a visit, creating an uncomfortable conversation that most of us, even children, wanted to avoid. "You're old enough to know better," was quoted not only to children.

Hard pews preceded the padded pews which emerged in the seventies in the city churches. Some church leaders felt that a proper repentance could not be generated sitting with posterior in a cushion wooed by the temptations of the world. One wondered if the Holy Spirit had to work twice the endeavor with padded pews. So, pine it was, hard pine, varnished and waxed weekly so that children, with a sideways exertion could slide 15 feet with limited effort. Sprayed with polish and scrubbed would make a slip and slide the likes of which were only beaten by water in some big city park. The children had long pews to crouch, hit, and slide facedown the entire length, banging the top of the head at the end like a cymbal to end the ride.

Most attendees, likely, did not know that Christianity existed many years while standing in worship. After the Reformation, sermons became a centerpiece and the congregation was forced to sit due to the length that evolved with the spoken Word.

Tobacco had not assumed its rightful place in the hazardous sins yet. It was free to soldiers in the military. Many farmer families received a government allotment of tobacco which translated into dollars at harvest time. For this reason, the cigarette was omitted from most sermons.

However, it was present on Sunday, usually in the break between Sunday School and Worship, smoked on the front lawn with great esteem and clouds of smoke drifting across the façade of the building. Filters were rare and destroyed some of the good flavor so they were frowned upon. The last puff was taken, the cigarettes tossed into the flower beds and the deacons resumed their pious position on the pews, hastily entering the building as the service started.

Service men in the armed forces received free packs on their pillows at night. Nobody knew it could kill them graveyard dead and turn their lungs into a mass of black tissue. This information came later, too late for many. In the early 1960's, most preachers, if they smoked at all, began to quit. Smoking moved closer to the definition of harming the "temple of the Holy Spirit," the human body. Sermons began mentioning this unhealthy act and lung cancer as well became diagnosed in members. The prayer list started containing names of those suffering with breathing issues from pulmonary disease and lung cancer came into vogue.

A symbolic nail in the coffin occurred on January 11, 1964 when Luther Terry, M.D., Surgeon General, released a report indicating that smoking is a cause of lung and esophageal cancer. The Cigarette Labeling and Advertising Act was passed in 1965. Cigarette packs were allowed to delay the warning until 1971.

The Methodists seemed to have a more relaxed interpretation of their eternal state. It was rumored that a prominent Methodist had a beer at some retreat, but this was unconfirmed. Beer with the Baptists, and most other church groups, if consumed, was in closed, quiet, private quarters. Never in a rowdy, bar, unless it was far in the country, off the beaten path of travel. A back door would be available and a booth in the corner would be commandeered. Caps were worn, dark clothing, nothing memorable. The staff accommodated with absolute privacy for the Christians who wanted an occasional drink, but did not keep the bottles in their homes. It was seen as more of a minor sin when purchased out of somebody else's bottle. It could be done in a more civilized fashion in a members' only club across town with some restrictions on prying eyes.

One of these public dens of iniquity, as they were colloquially called, had an unexpected visitor one Saturday night. A reveler backed an old truck to the front door of the juke joint and sent a wild hog in, as he closed and locked the door behind the beast. The hog rooted and grunted, knocking tables and chairs asunder, as patrons in a state of hazed fog from alcohol and cigarettes screamed and exited. It was said a back door was made where nary was one. It was the only time in the establishment history where more left in a minute than came in all night.

Catholics used real wine in communion and freely periodically confessed their sins, aloud to the priest. This seemed to imply a more tolerant outlook on alcohol and most of us liked this interpretation immensely. The idea of a private confessional booth was very intriguing to those of us who had grown up with some manner of repentance on the front row of the church in front of God and everybody.

"Tell it all brother", had likely been said too many times. It brought forth responses which varied from uncouth to pure sin that nobody needed to know about. In a resurrection sermon that gestured for public participation, one energetic member confessed, "I dug up a dead man once, he was yellow as a pumpkin." This invoked no follow-up discussion from the group and the sentence just hung in the air.

A gossiping member would repeat another's transgression as a dramatic event, addressed to a group of men at a town restaurant. Being assured of the attention it would garner, these sessions were thoroughly addictive as the men waited with baited breath for additional information. "I saw the response card." one solemnly related, "it was worse than what he confessed." "The man and the woman went forward to the same mourner's bench." another related, "inches from each other". The waitress would then repeat bits and pieces of what she heard to other patrons. The more pious the member, the more clout the gossip carried. By the end of the day, what started out as a tale of minor indiscretions morphed into full blooded sin with damnation. The preacher was quoted that, "he had never seen anything like it.", another spouted that "Sodom and Gomorrah were no worse." as he waged a finger and peered through black studious glasses. As teenagers, we came to believe that confession might or might not be good for the soul.

Party telephone lines with multiple homes helped spread the sins. Listening became professional with ability to click into the conversation and not be detected. A confessional in a booth behind a screen seemed to be a much better solution with less chance of public embellishment by the members, who watched the front row, trying to read the sinner's lips as they counseled with the preacher. Perhaps the priest had less interest in telling the school authorities or our parents. He was bound with only God and himself to know the sin. This sounded practical. A Catholic girl told us that the priest was bound by law to not ever tell anyone what we confessed, even our parents or a school principal. This sounded very satisfying and relaxing. We wondered if us non-Catholics could confess to the priest and not have to reveal anything to our parents of our dastardly deeds of delinquency.

After a rousing sermon, a confessional incident at a local Baptist group involved girls confessing their "skinny dipping" from the front row. In their totally repented, contrite state, they confessed the names of the boys that assisted them in the sinful endeavor. This resulted in a large blow up of congregational proportions. Parents intended to find the chief suspects who had made their angels fall from grace. The effort was pointless as the blame appeared to be universal to all parties.

A member of one church claimed that he had recognized a local preacher at a Ku Klux Klan rally by a large slit in eyeholes on his hood. The member felt the preacher shouldn't have been there, but apparently felt that members could attend, if not recognized. When the tale was told to wiser people, the rumor or fact died on the vine. It was said that the perpetrator sewed up the eyes of his hood a little tighter.

This was in the time when some blacks and whites hated each other. This was certainly not universal as churches preached on love to the fellow man. As with a lot of the Bible, some members just did not obey it.

School desegregation was a rumble on the track. We, as children began to see incidents and public opposition, which differed from the sermon content that we were hearing at church about kindness. John Kennedy, in 1963, was responsible for the integration of University of Alabama, in spite of opposition from George Wallace, the Governor. Kennedy gave a nationally televised speech concerning civil rights. A civil rights activist, Medgar Evers was killed the next day at his home in Mississippi. In 1975, 3 years after being paralyzed, Governor Wallace apologized for his behavior to black groups and Civil Rights associations. Southern raising taught us to apologize when we knew we were wrong.

An evening knock at the principal's home revealed a shabbily dressed, alcohol laced, red faced man espousing that the problem was my father who was responsible for the blacks and whites soon to merge at the elementary school. "You could have prevented it.", the intoxicated man said as he yelled racial epithets. The conversation went nowhere. The man parted with, "I will go to hell before my child goes to school with "one of them." My dad closed the door, addressed my mother, brother and myself, and with a solemn face and said "yes, he will".

A Christian lady in her carport addressed one of the KKK, as they were called, and said, "the Bible says we are to love our neighbor and our fellow man." "Why are you doing this?" He lowered his head and walked away, and drove off. He had to know, in his heart, that this was not right. It took many years for him and others to admit it.

I WILL TAKE IT ON THE POACH

"I will take it on the poach," Tom said, to my grandmother, as he stood outside the screen door that led into the kitchen. She was urging Tom, as she did frequently, to come into the kitchen and eat with us, my grandparents and myself. The dinner bell had been rung; the workers were dismissed for lunch. Tom stayed in the area and ate on the porch. He never would accept the invitation to come into the home.

I was 7 years old in 1960 and I wanted Tom to come inside as well. It was a small table against the wall on the porch, it was literally six feet from our table, where I normally ate with my grandparents. My grandparents offered it, he always declined. His mantra after the offer was always, "I will take it on the poach." Tom was a black man.

In those days, there were black and white-water fountains, bathrooms, cafeterias, and schools, the separate but equal policy. My cousin and I had a joke which we would propagate at the local courthouse, trying to drink out of the water fountains labeled "colored" with a black and white sign placed above the white fixture, as our parents looked keenly at the two renegades.

I guess Tom could not make the six-foot leap, even if invited. It was a distance he could not traverse. He would have felt an aberration or a wrinkle in his life. He felt secure, I now assume, in the status quo. Why rock the boat? Was it fear or the routine that he felt that he had to keep? Was it just too much, to even accept kindness, in a world that had drawn deep lines of separation? Would he face punishment from somebody? It was a short six-foot distance, but mentally, a long journey of a lifetime.

Disappointed again, I ate lunch at the table with my grandparents. Silverware could be heard lightly clinking and clanging intermittently from both sides of the screen door. We could not see each other, the minor noise seemed to be a competition between the tables. It was bizarre, noise coming from two sites, yet neither could see the other. It was as if silverware was communicating in some manner.

I was smart, yet childish and ignorant of any racial lines, at my age. I knew there was something amiss in this arrangement. It was one of those childhood memories where you have puzzled concern, but you do not really know what it means. It was decades before I put it all together in some disjointed solution that still made no sense. My grandmother always insisted, but Tom never ate with us. I look back on her now as the true hero of the event, trying to do what was right, in perilous times.

I was mesmerized by his dark hands, yellowed eyes, and slow drawl. I followed him around the field where he worked, watching him sweat profusely, and hanging on every word, which were few and far between. His mind was on corn or okra or livestock when he worked, not some kid coming at his heels. After a day's work, granddaddy carried him home in the pickup truck, over the railroad track, to the quarters where he lived in a meager abode. I wedged myself between Tom and my grandfather, wanting to be close to both. My legs straggled the gear stick. This was repeated many times. I would say, loudly, "move over Tom." and Tom would laugh loudly and repeat the phrase.

The farm was a hundred acres, purchased in 1917 for 35 $ an acre, providing sustenance for four children and two adults, as well as a set of grandparents. Food was plentiful and grown, cultivated, and tended, to provide the daily meal. One mule occupied the land, sometimes two. They lived in the barn and ate corn stored in the corn crib throughout the year. Two tobacco barns dotted the landscape and side work areas allowed stringing during the season, as the sleds brought in the tobacco drawn by mules and then tractors.

Prior to the purchase of the land in 1917, my grandfather had been drafted into World War 1, he contracted Spanish flu, spent a year on a cot in a Detroit Hospital, and survived. Many died. He recovered, was discharged, lungs damaged, and sharecropped on land, until the farm of a hundred acres could be purchased, a few miles down the road.

My grandfather was a kind and gentle man. He was known to make coffins in the barn for both black and white residents of the county. He was a minister and farmer, performing funerals for black residents in the area. He remembered a poignant service, where he eulogized a young child of a black worker. After the service, the mother insisted on paying him. My grandfather refused, but she took his hand and placed coins in the palm. He opened the palm and it held a nickel and two pennies. His eyes always moistened when he told the story, of how the mother wanted peace and dignity. He kept the 7 cents and allowed her to have that dignity. Blacks and whites worked together on the "place," as land was termed, in those years. They developed deep friendships.

In 1921, my grandfather, at the urging of this wife, Elizabeth, went to college. She had been to college and was a teacher. He took, both his wife and newly born son, to Tennessee. He left the purchased land with his father, Preston Beauregard Chapman, to be tended. This itself was a leap of faith to leave behind a farm that was mortgaged to the Scottish Land Company. His remaining father would produce the note payment based on crop production. He still owed 1500 dollars on the land; the total had been 3500 dollars.

They chose a Christian college in Nashville, Tennessee named David Lipscomb. When he arrived, it was learned that he did not have enough high school credits to enter the college. He attended David Lipscomb High School in the first year, in order to matriculate into the college a year later. Some would have taken the train home. He did not. He maintained this fortitude and determination throughout his life and returned to South Georgia to work and live out the attributes and kindness that he had learned, farming, showing kindness throughout the community and teaching in churches in the area.

After his death, I learned, that my grandfather, Adair Pinckney Chapman, (1889-1978), was named after one of his grandfathers, who died years before he was born, Charles Pinckney (1757-1824). Pinckney was a planter and signer of the Constitution from Charleston, South Carolina. Unknowingly, grandchildren have lived the last few years close to

Pinckneyville Middle School in an area of Georgia, initially called Pinckneyville, now named Norcross. Pinckney loved the area and made several trips there from Charleston, South Carolina.

VISITORS IN THE SANCTUARY

The three men entered the church unannounced and unobtrusively, not illegally, but during regular business hours, a service being conducted on a Wednesday night. They came in close to starting time, a little late to be given any prolonged greetings or particulars. They entered quietly, at the appropriate time, taking a seat closer to the front, on the end of a pew, that had never been claimed by any members. Pews were traditionally staked out by regulars in southern churches and it was unheard of to uproot some little white-haired widow who had sat on the pew for 50 years, intermittently, of course. In some churches, actual plaques were on a pew, indicating the appropriate family ownership during the worship services. Pews could be sold to provide additional funds for the work of the church. This was not uncommon.

Each visiting man had a bible and wore no ties since it was a night service in the middle of the week. In 1968, their attendance would not be unusual in any manner, except for one biological reason, the color of their skin. The men were black and this was a southern town of 10,000. They sat quietly and sang the songs, bowed heads for prayer, but offered no commentary in the adult class. They were not called on to provide any supportive scriptural interpretations.

I was 13, mildly surprised, but not shocked at their attendance. I knew the men, as I had attended a revival at their black church years earlier. They were involved in leadership at their church. I couldn't quit eyeing them during the service, wondering what would happen, if anything. I didn't expect anyone to utter a harsh word, but the action itself led to curiosity. The service ended. Hands were shaken, smiles advanced, and conversation realized. Apparently, the men left satisfied with no explanations.

Thirty-five years later, I was in a nursing home and came across one of the three men, bedridden due to age and medical conditions. He could not speak due to a stroke. He looked at me and our eyes locked. He smiled this sincere, kind, knowing smile, and I knew that he knew who I was, the preacher's kid. I took his hand and we exchanged a deep stare knowing exactly what the other was thinking. He gave me a smile, a head nod and we parted, two brothers in this old world, friends forever, locked by a service on a Wednesday night, where nobody objected to a black man walking into a white church.

Years later, I realized what a good influence this was on me at my age. To see the fellowship with no adverse effects was helpful to my development. Church taught that kindness was due all, but in this instance, it was acted out right there in front of me. It was not uncommon in that era for churches within the business meeting to pass some ordinance or recommendation to not allow black members to join. Sometimes the attendance of a different skin color caused a commotion unbefitting a group supposedly ascribing to Christianity.

Ten years later, 1976, a black man from Albany, Ga was denied entering the Plains Baptist Church by a closed, locked door, a few days before the election of President Carter. The black men arrived on this particular Sunday morning and the door was locked, service cancelled. The church had been advised by phone that the trio would be attending worship, a hastily cancelled service was suddenly deemed necessary to prevent the action.

Weeks before the election, President Carter was located on the campaign trail in Houston, Texas, where he voiced objection to what had transpired back home in Plains. The incident was quite publicized and President Carter had opposed the ruling that prohibited blacks in the church years earlier.

ROBBERY OF THE COMMUNION MAN

It was a big city church, asphalt parking lot, no mud to soil suits. stained glass, huge air conditioner systems, educational wing, large flannel boards with stick figures for the masses. There were large benevolence programs, a radio show, a large vacation bible school, two revivals a year. A long black Cadillac always had a parking place on the side closest to a door, a tribute to a wonderful member who always gave the kids Juicy Fruit gum. The Gum Man. This member would frequently ride with the minister in the car behind the hearse on the way to the cemetery. He commented, "Someday we will be at the front of the line just like him." as he pointed to the casket visible through the back window of the hearse. "We need to be ready." He spoke. The two contemplated as the hearse bounced along in front of them.

Today, it was rather spooky, shadows flittering over the pews as the wind howled outside and limited light filtered through big stained-glass windows on a

Saturday. Shapes and shadows materialized at the floor and walls. They moved with the jerky bursts of wind outside. It was a big city church, money, influence and big buildings. Faith on steroids. Members with muscle.

The boy crept along the sides of the pew and ambushed his cousin carrying the communion, lunging into the pew space, a blow to the back, communion tray grabbed and entire unleavened bread tray and cup tray carried off down the aisle. It was a planned execution of "Robbery of the Communion Man". It was played out in the empty churches, as the preacher's kid found keys and used the premises when no one was around. One supposedly, unsuspecting participant, carrying communion to 200 invisible worshippers, only to be attacked in the middle of the staid service for purposes of violence and mayhem. The main perp shouting "act like you're surprised." "A tumble ensued and immediately the communion was absconded, only to meet later in the lobby of the darkened building where toasts were made of the ill-gotten gain and stale grape juice, certainly not drinkable, went down the gullet of the participants.

Most of the time it was all imaginary, but the enterprise was crystalized when the boys found real communion bread and occasionally mold- tinged grape juice. This elevated the entire experience to a new level and the perps were confident if caught, they would be exonerated with one Bible verse. They knew the story of David stealing shewbread in the temple when hungry. No problem. This certainly justified the deed. Who doesn't want to be like David, a man after God's own heart?

It was not breaking and entering, the door to the Baptist church was unlocked. It sat adjacent to the elementary school, with salvation a hundred yards from the monkey bars and swings. The cousins were caught by the parents, one pounding the piano like Jerry Lee Lewis and one screaming from the pulpit like a Pentecostal preacher, engaged in their own service with invisible members coming forward to confess transgressions. The pair was apprehended, one spanked unmercifully and the other placed at a desk copying Bible verses about unlawful breaking and entering. This soothed the conscience of the parents, but did little to remove this Tom Sawyer attitude of attacking juvenile delinquency with a passion unmatched by most restrained individuals. These were preacher's kids, doing their best to live up to the expected behavior at school and at church.

The biggest offense or blessing, depending on which side of the law you were on, was swimming in the baptistry. Generally, the door was locked, that key was unfindable. It would be hidden, not on a key ring but on a special nail mounted much too high for a ten-year-old delinquent.

The town baptistries were built after rivers became unfashionable and danger was realized when using the local creeks or ponds. Big city churches had this option early as the big city church had no available body of water. The baptistries were built for function, not show or prominence. It was a narrow pool with steps so high, steep and elevated, that a stumble would lead to a sinking.

In one instance, the preacher was absent and a member elected to baptize his friend. Both were unfamiliar with the procedure in the room. The pair thought that each should put on a pair of waders that were hanging on hooks. When the curtains parted, the congregation beheld each in waders, both in the water. As the dunking occurred, both waders quickly filled with water making exit difficult. The church witnessed two resembling salamanders crawling on all fours up the steep steps out of the baptistry. Stunned silence delayed the curtain puller until the pair were at the top step and the curtain slammed shut. The recently baptized told the preacher the next Sunday, "I wish that I had waited on you, he tried to drown me."

One volunteer assembling communion on a Saturday, for the service the next day, became disoriented and stepped through the small narrow door. Instead of finding a communion closet of supplies, she found the top step of the baptistry and plunged headfirst into the ice-cold water. She foundered, flipped, flopped and somehow removed herself from drowning and made haste to her car to go home to change clothes. She returned to the duties of communion preparation. By the grace of God, the preacher was in his yard at the parsonage across the street and saw her drenched and departing from the premises and additionally saw her return 15 minutes later in dry clothes. He hastily went across the street and confronted her, asking if he could help her. She told the story, embarrassed, but glad to survive. She begged him not to tell anyone, but he said, "I'm sorry, "this is too good not to tell."

For a juvenile to be caught in the baptistry was dangerous because there was a penalty that would certainly involve the rod and the child. This was generally avoided and the only remembrance that I have was once in a small church which had no lock on the baptistry door. We had provided swim suits for the occasion and were afraid to stay long. The water was never that clean anyway, it was water with stale chlorine, so we did not linger.

After hours, it was the balcony that held the

greatest ability to conjure up a spooky, scary, story about some lost individual, wandering the halls of churches, bumping up the balcony steps to blast with horror and screaming into the invisible worshippers, something about the search for a golden arm, thus far avoiding recovery. The balcony was especially dark after hours, the steps angled, the seats were sloped. It was the perfect entry for an impersonation of an unsaved Jack the Ripper looking for blood. Even the most seasoned juvenile delinquent could become pale and sweaty in the darkness at the screaming and the sounds of bumps and moans, knowing it was pure fakery but not feeling any safer.

COMMUNION, JESUS AND FANTA

The sermon had been presented, the sinners called, blessings given and the communion was proceeding. The bread had been broken, passed, eaten, and the plates returned, orderly, to the front table, where upon lay the inscription, "Do This in Remembrance of Me". We all knew who the Me was. We knew the Bible did say when to take it, by the simple word, "Often". There was no time or day commandment, it was done by examples and inferences of the early Church, who participated on other days as well as the first day of the week. We knew the early Church had the memorial known as the Lord's Supper. We know that Paul chastised the Corinthians for getting drunk at the associated fellowship meal and mistreating those of lessor stature. He gave a stern warning about what the meal and service entailed. It was supposed to bring back the remembrance of the Covenant that Jesus had established in the Upper Room the night before he was crucified when he changed the liturgy of the

Passover with his disciples to a new format and then arose from the dead three days later.

This day, in a little country church, as the wine or emblem or juice, or sacrament, as it is called, was passed, there was a sudden silent, but slightly audible "uh oh" quietly heard from some woman in the midst of the passage. Discreet and soft, she was never identified. It came from some distant pew toward the front of the church. The origin was undiscoverable. It could have been a spilled cup or some other mild calamity, perhaps some communion cups had not been filled. I had seen that lead to a quick exit and a return after a filling of more cups, but this was different.

I lurched sideways to receive my tray of which to select a small cup. Heads in the group looked down as usual, but something was amiss. Glass cups rattled as usual when placed empty back into the metal trays. There were no disposable cups until the mid-1970's. The heads were a little lower bowed than usual. I partook, "take ye all of it" as Jesus said, so I drained the three milliliters in the cup. Tasted different, as it hit my tongue and slightly burned. I knew immediately, it was carbonated, but the right color. Then it hit me, "Fanta" grape was in my cup. I grinned like a Cheshire Cat. I recognized it before I swallowed, I gasped and gulped as it shot down my gullet burning-, since it was in an unrefrigerated state. Had it been ice cold, many might not have noticed it, especially 75-year-old taste buds. An adult mistake, I loved it. It seemed to give me some satisfaction and pacify my need for mischief for a period of time.

Somebody didn't or couldn't find grape juice or didn't know it mattered and bought a big bottle of Fanta Grape off the shelf at Winn Dixie. It was used in the Lord's Supper preparation. At least the right color,

50 % correct. Flavor 20%. The hour passed, the
service ended, no comments, no critique at the
church, at least until the family dinner table. My dad
had some responsibility to decide what kind of act this
was. Was it a perpetrator exercising a criticism of the
crucifixion? Was it a debauchery and mockery of the
Sacraments? Was somebody bound to a Fanta's hell?
No, he decided. It was a member who in good faith
was trying to work and provide a service and in the
Deep South, Fanta was grape juice, sort of, almost
like, almost. The event was quietly forgotten and the
misinformed, a Godly widow, was advised to buy
grape juice but was not chastised in any way. No blind
fold with a shooting at sunrise. No harsh words about
corrupting the blood of Jesus with carbonated water.
No flogging or unmasking or doxing, just a quiet
comment. No excommunication. I did wonder what
would have happened if the servant had gotten way
out of line and just used wine in those little cups. Now
that would have gotten some attention, biblical for
sure, but what a dramatic noon meal discussion that
would have been.

Most of us are not theologians in the Church, nor
do we have to be. It is not likely the prostitute at the
well held a good understanding of the Sovereignty of
God, or the sacraments or doctrine or the genealogy of
Jesus, the Jewish rabbi. But she was forgiven, that's
all she cared about, and forgiven by the son who could
forgive her, right then, right now, in her dirty, sweaty,
unforgiven state. She came the dirty way to Jesus,
which Jesus admitted was the way we all come, even if
we are clean by soap standards.

There's a pharisaical tendency to think lower of
those who have not been handed the platter of faith
from a Eunice or Lois like some have, or those who
have not attended and studied at the feet of

theologians or basked in apologetics with professors. We can look at those who came to Jesus and marvel at how bad they needed it, while ignoring our own discretions, similar to the member who told the preacher, "You really told them today, preacher."

Certainly, God has children but no grandchildren and each must work out his own salvation with the fear that accompanies it. We are not taken into God's grace from a relative or neighbors' faith or teachers' faith regardless of how great that faith may have been or how genetically we have been connected to the faith giver. The most grateful in the Bible, Jesus said, were the ones who needed him the most, the sick who needed a physician.

There's us, fallen man, who must humbly recognize that we are of this nature. There is then the basic need, which is God, which Romans says is self-evident. Then, the basic need of forgiveness from God, offered by Jesus, the Son of God. These are the roots of the tree of life. Then, if we solve that problem of our humanity and if we have the energy, we can then battle over the size of the stained glass in the foyer, or the tile, or coffee in the building, or loudness of instruments or vocals in an Assembly or the size of the Sanctuary, or the bank note on all of it, or the use of the church money to give to causes, or the parking lot size or the light bulbs in the auditorium or the odd color of the outdoor carpet in the fellowship hall or the member who contributes a few dollars a month but drives a luxury automobile and parks that car in a most desirable spot, every service.

It is no grand surprise that mega churches sprang up in the last 40 years with an attempt to mobilize a call to a Joy of Jesus, unfettered by the social class or strata of society, with ties shed, uniforms removed and a liturgy that propelled the service of man, the justice and love of God, and the removal of sins to the forefront, maintained by the level ground at the foot of the Cross, where all were welcomed.

SWEATING FOR JESUS

The Christian perspired as he used a wrench on a jammed door. Another was on his back attaching a brace to a pulpit in the auditorium. Another changed out and installed new tile in the educational wing. It was a church workday. Some were retired, others off work from their jobs for the day. These were volunteers, workers assigned a task that normally would cost the church money. They were members, merely using their expertise to repair and service. These were church projects, needed tasks that had to be done. The church would not be charged for any of the repairs. This was standard thought in 1965.

There were more activities in the kingdom than saving souls, preaching the good news and recording in the bulletin the names of the saved. Even the deacons in the New Testament were formed for tasks. It was widows in that instance. They were hungry and the problem was solved by appointment of the deacons.

Throughout Christendom for hundreds of years, somebody had to cut on the lights, cut off the lights, mow the grass, clean up and tend to the nursery, shine the pews while cleaning the church, putting up Easter or Christmas decorations, emptying trash from the class rooms, scrubbing crayon stain off furniture, pew repair, floor cleaning and on and on. The work never ceased and was divided among volunteers. Keys were plentiful and work always continued. Whomever had the new riding lawn mower was respectfully asked if he would try it out on the lawn, in a regular manner.

Certainly, no one was paid to clean the building. That would be a sacrilege, an abomination, something that could split a church wide open, as they say. It was the Lord's money and churches were careful with it. With all the able-bodied men available, it would be foolish to bring up a firm in the business meeting to perform such tasks. The Lord's money could not be spent frivolously or wasted. That was the thought, at least until the mid - 1970's.

Churches came to believe it would be much easier to pay a nursery worker or a service man on the heating system. A lawn service could trim the hedges and cut the grass much more efficiently than volunteers who were accused by the esthetic members of using a butchering low blade on the mower scraping into the dirt and edges of flower beds.

It became a moot point with no angry discussions. Culture evolved. Times changed. Mankind would work during the week, but not on their off time at a building or sanctuary. Off time was for hunting, fishing, family activities, golf, and other interests. Hence, pianists were hired, nursery workers, painters, cleaners, managers of flooring, youth directors for the youth, when previously it was a volunteer job for those with patience and low tempers.

It was in vogue now to hire workers for the Lord's maintenance. To those that had been tasked with labor, it was a welcome relief. A few thought that it was a waste of the treasury but didn't complain as that could lead to an assignment of volunteer work. Times were good and contribution would be used for these endeavors.

THE URGENCY OF LIFE

The suit in place, the preacher loosened his tie with a twist of his fingers and addressed the congregation. Loudly, he began. I speak today on the urgency of life; the baby comes out kicking and screaming, an observer cannot tell initially which direction the baby wants. He seems to want to stay in his warm, comfortable place. Then suddenly, he changes his mind, and demands exit. He signals some muscle contraction similar to beating on a closed door, the pelvic muscles oblige and spit out the baby like a visual thrust into the world, entered in great confusion and unknown fear. The mother screams or bites her lip, sweat falls, tears, fluids, motions of distress, and there's the infant. It all becomes urgent, urgently getting out of the amnionic fluid, urgently entering a world of life. The doctor has padded the floor in case a slick infant comes out to fast.

A birth score is taken a couple of times, the infant is measured, poked, prodded and touched, toes and fingers are counted, and the baby goes to the mother's chest and the baby seems at peace. The mother smiles. The father waits in the lobby, of course, in the 1960's and 1970's, the father is generally not in the labor room. They are all united within the hour, provided no complications. It was all urgent, the ride to the hospital, the labor, the delivery, the care at the hospital. All a matter of utmost urgency.

We begin that day at our birth, living life as an urgent entrance into a world, that seems to invite us to jump in, hold on, and take it as it comes and to never look back.

There are some aspects that are missing from this entrance. The secular world tells us to pull up our bootstraps, level our shoulders and stand tall to face the obstacles. This is not bad advice; however, we are called to accomplish a task, a life, a mission. God, the afterthought, is rarely mentioned by the world. It is the parent's responsibility to raise the child, not the state or community. If God is absent at the home, it is possible that this entrant into the world will miss God as well.

The preacher continues, we maintain the urgency of education, the urgent job search, the urgency of growing up, without the urgency of worshipping the God who made this entrance into the world possible and who, according to Paul, "we live and move and maintain our being."

The preacher moves on to the works of Satan, who is referred to by name. He relates that Satan can say a prayer, act nice, wear a suit and tie, sit on the front row, even recount with great gusto the prayers of a sinner, or even be baptized, the preacher relates that he has seen all of it. But there is one thing the devil cannot and will not ever do, that is- repent. He will never turn back, he may relent, the preacher maintains, but never repent. Satan will never apologize for his actions, never change, never start over, never have prayers and supplications to God.

There is, he maintained, urgency of life, but folks, fellow Christians, there is the certainty of death, where we will be judged. Everyone on that judgement day will bow and confess Jesus as the Son of God. There is the urgency of accountability. Accountability is coming, as we will be held accountable for all we have done in this life. Do not wait folks, for that last day, for that day when time will be no more, when it is too late to confess. Do it today with urgency, with purpose, with obedience. Pull up the bootstraps and do this, not filled with pride but humble before the God of the Bible.

"We should live in urgency.", the preacher admonished. Then he advises the flock to urgently seek Jesus, the Son of God and his Word. To seek first, not last, and not without urgency, the Kingdom of God. The congregation listens, in rapt attention, and several crowd the front row during the invitation song amid the call to the front. Sunday morning is winding down. It is the usual crowd, no Easter Lilies or Poinsettias, the designation that some have given to those Christians who come only on Easter or Christmas.

Hands are shaken at the front door, admonitions proudly stated to the preacher, "you really told them today, preacher." one man said, possibly indicating the sermon was applicable to everyone but him.

The only thing left by lunch time was the dissecting of the minister's sermon which could happen at a dinner table, in the congregation within the hour. What did he mean by that? Can you believe his audacity? The verdict would be, hopefully for the preacher, acceptable for his continued service in the little church, and not having stepped on too many toes. Hopefully, a committee meeting with complaints would not be eminent. A slip of the tongue, a remark received the wrong way, could derail a preacher. Complaints from a large contributor, though certainly not biblically more important than anyone else, were a concern.

This was a consideration that Jesus did not endure. He was the Son of God and he wasn't concerned about offending the proud. They were all dirty as far as the world and he was the only way out with the abundant life. He told them point blank, in their robes, garb, and studies of the scripture tied to their garments. The Pharisees wouldn't even let John the Baptist baptize them. They didn't want to be splashed with dirty water that sinners had contacted. They maintained that they, the leaders of the synagogue, were the pious one, the ones from Israel who knew who was clean, and who was dirty. They also blasted Jesus at dinner tables, but in the end, they crucified him.

In fact, Jesus's dinner table was filled with sinners, tax collectors, harlots, and those of the world, those deeply entrenched in the ways of the world, knowing that what they did was wrong. They were convicted. It was "those people" who the religious zealots hated and treated unclean and avoided. It was Jesus' association with them that caused his death, one of the reasons. "He communed with sinners", the Pharisees said.

After the masses, the socially unimportant, the poor, the bereaved, saw Jesus, and his purity, which they accepted. The realization came to those worldly people, that something was missing in their lives. Jesus pointed this out to them at a table of fellowship and then received them, with their obedience, into his kingdom. Jesus died for that, fighting against the religious zealots till the day he was crucified on a hill called Golgotha. They never got the point, their robes and attire were too thick, too maintained, covered by their scriptures, too separated from the world. This hill, though elevated, was actually level at the foot of the Cross, for all those dirty sinners to come and be received. But, the more religious of the day, would not receive his invitation.

PASS THE LEMONADE

The entire summer package of the South included gnats, mosquitoes at dusk, lightning bugs, and sultry sunsets. The farmer sweated hard thought the summer. Crops were coming in, and with it, funds to survive another year, hopefully. One grandchild later described it as, "scratching out a meager existence from unyielding dirt." This was an accurate description. There was no pivot system of irrigation, for most, except what God deemed relevant to send from the sky. In this mixture of heat, struggle, work, duress, came VBS, the central activity of the Christian summer. Like the fall meeting, Vacation Bible School was a mainstay of the local church. It sparked twinkles in children's eyes as memories of songs, candy and crafts dominated the memory.

The larger churches of the towns had elaborate programs from hours of committee meetings. They had unlimited new flannel boards with characters that appropriately stuck, ample construction paper, larger gallons of lemonade, larger more stable cups, and scissors for each participant- no shared scissors. Glue was used by the case, the squirt kind, glue sticks were an anomaly. Beads were glued by the thousands to activity boards expressing a message, "Go ye." Popsicle sticks provided multiple ways to build a craft. Mobility was needed. The volunteer had to march. Songs were sung, but combined with marching, running, stepping high, clapping, yelling, and that final ear jarring shout, before Jericho fell. Dogs that licked the sores of Lazarus were treated to smeared peanut butter on a volunteer who lay still as the dog licked. The most memorable dog was a gargantuan German Shepherd that looked threatening, but licked peacefully, the elbows and back, with not much ado. The children screamed with delight and horror, pointing, and observing from a distance, scared out of their minds but never forgetting this Vacation Bible School.

Little hands in all congregations spilled the unstable lemonade cups onto the seating of the low tables, engineered in some cases with the teacher sitting in the center, surrounded by toddlers, a u-shaped arrangement invented for that purpose.

The event usually ran mornings for a week in the early years, sometimes migrating to a few evenings a week when the volunteers were less active. Early VBS ran a solid week, Sunday through Friday. Awards were given on Friday for memory work and other activities.

This was hard core work, VBS, before the advent of so many Christian songs and bands that are now used in the endeavor. It has now become an industry with themed Vacation Bible School throughout the church groups, but it had its origins where members had to originate the theme and provide the labor.

To look down with derision on the ancient VBS is a

mistake. These were the formative skeletal years of the VBS that is seen today with its glitzy costumes, actual actors, music from great singers. Every activity has to have an origin. This was the foundation of the current modern VBS- the grass roots of the modern extravaganza.

In 1965, the children entered bright eyed and eager to learn, and left with ribbons and metals and Bibles and sheets with the names of the 12 apostles, even Judas, as well as crafts of much variety. It was the highlight of a church summer. It was the foundation for the future of which was a sliver of the whole Christian experience, lemonade for all, wholesome activities, and lifelong friendships.

PROPS AND ILLUSTRATIONS

He was a stocky fellow, thick chested, almost muscular, wearing a suit and a tie. Starting at one end of the pulpit, he trudged across, the cross on his back, shoulders bent. His face was gnarled, sweat dropping, as he screamed loudly, echoing around the auditorium, "What are you going to do with the cross of Jesus tonight?" He would limp across a few more steps, sagging under the weight, and repeat the question, loudly. The audience was spellbound, uncomfortable and perspiring like the preacher. He was walking slow; how long could this go on? Where was he going? Would he walk down the aisle? Would a Simon appear and take up the cross? Should a concerned, energetic member bolt to the front and say, "I will carry the cross for Jesus." They mulled all this over and felt both convicted and very uncomfortable.

The crowd had never seen a minister in the role as actor, symbolically carrying the cross of Jesus, which was not present. The back was slumped, the shoulders sagged, but the cross was invisible. It was not there. It was a memorable sermon, and one of the first seen with an invisible prop in mid-1960's. This was not common. Drama was minimal in 1960, other than in the men's business meetings.

In the latter part of the 60's and into 70's, communication courses developed and colleges offered speech classes as curriculum. Communication and speech became a discipline of learning and training in the college degree process. Professional speech writers and to some extent sermon writers evolved. This culture bled over into the sermons that were delivered on Sunday. Most considered it a positive step. It was thought to assist in the transformation of a dull speaker into a popular presenter of the Faith.

Props became common with the arrival in the 70's of the youth minister or children/family ministry programs. Preachers tried to become more vibrant, there were Toastmasters Clubs, Dale Carnegie Courses and speech courses geared toward the ministry. It seemed that with training, a failure could be exciting. It was all in the annunciation and cadence of voice.

Jesus had props, he would look at a mountain or a child or Jerusalem, the city, and pronounce a sermon. He used the widow's mite, a returning son, or a sick person to teach a lesson. But that was Jesus, not mortals. The use of props was controversial in some circles. It was a fine line. Paul had clearly said in 1 Corinthians 2:1-5 that he had not come with eloquent speaking, but with fear, trembling and weakness preaching only Jesus Christ and him crucified.

The more dramatic personalities could conjure up swinging from a rope into the auditorium, landing, if lucky, at the pulpit. All manner of artifacts and jars filled with anything from worms to mustard seeds to enlighten the audience could make the encounter memorable. A well-researched lesson could certainly have points added with symbols that might call to mind the lesson later. One well trained preacher, who had majored in Speech, brought a Stratovarius violin which he allowed to be passed around the congregation. Amazingly, it was not dropped or broken in transit between the pews. It did have an impact.

Some complained that the Holy Spirit was powerful enough and did not need a push or nudge beyond the pages of the scripture. Additions to some, seemed unnecessary and redundant. These innovations could drag out the lesson past lunch time. Others found props entertaining and the addition distracted them from the low-keyed preacher.

One preacher rolled a closed casket into the sanctuary, apparently, not advising any of the leadership of the congregation as to what was about to transpire. This was an addition with a shock effect. He then preached a sermon, walked out of the pulpit, and propped open the casket, asking the congregation to file by and pay respects to a person who had been a Christian, but had given up the faith. "Let us see what a dead congregation looks like." he said. As the reluctant congregation slowly walked by and peered expectantly into the casket, they were met with a full view of their own faces, as a mirror was in the bottom of the casket, instead of a body. As one would surmise, this demonstration had varying effects on people and was not completely received as a good addition to the lesson.

One athletically inclined minister juggled during the sermon and had a circuit revival of such. He would quote scripture and make sermon points as he flailed and leaped around the pulpit balancing milk jugs on varying parts of his body. This was received with some amusement, but no real interest.

Fake blood was not readily available, thus ketchup could be used and dripped onto a sword, for a presentation of the crucifixion. This was tried by a youth minister but with limited success and it tended to wind up on the notes and the Bible. Props were not without problems, one had to know exactly when to insert them into the sermon and when to remove. If it needed to be hidden, it needed to fit back into a pocket. It was not a good time to decide where to place the props while giving the lesson.

One of the first props on the podium was the chart, a large, square, bedsheet sized, cotton fabric that held the lesson in large black print. The entire sheet was covered up with a blank sheet during the singing. Until the minister started, the covering sheet was not removed. If a lesson was studied by the audience for an entire song service, one could lose interest quickly. The congregation was made curious when the lesson was exposed.

A popular chart lesson was, "The Christian Race", which showed a path and walkway that was attempting to get through life as he was attacked on the road with multiple problems and sins. The preacher, with a pointer, traveled with the Christian as he faced the obstacles.

One prop was two golf balls which symbolized some part of the Christian walk. However, the speaker had not realized that most podiums are more slanted than others, meaning the only place a golf ball could rest was in his pockets. He lamented that he had almost lost both props in the middle of the presentation, by balancing them at the top of the lectern. Gravity sent them rolling straight down. The sermon was interrupted when he had to twist and capture both rolling balls, as they leaped from the podium.

Another one of the props were simple handcuffs to indicate the bond of the wicked to Satan. The preacher would dangle them from the podium like a charm, slight clanging and clinking as they swayed. Others wore them, with great fanfare, the small key turning in the lock. This caused everyone in the room to silently gasp. It was a great picture of the snare of the devil and was a good illustration, unless a mechanism failed.

Prior to the late sixties, sound systems in auditoriums were rare. The sound was dependent on the volume of the preacher. Thus, he talked loudly and frequently and stayed hoarse from speaking. With the construction of new buildings, the sound systems were grand and loud. However, one instance revealed that the sound system received all the police and emergency calls during the sermon. This caused a fifteen-minute wild listening experience, when a fire alarm was called in on some building in town. The preacher comprehended what was happening and turned off the sound system, as the congregation started getting more interested in police calls than Jesus.

The construction of the new buildings was set so that the masses could enter and leave out the front double door. Side entrances were required due to fire hazards but these were small exits difficult for large families or wheelchairs to accommodate. Teenagers would invariably try to escape from those side exits. One determined member locked the side doors, and hid the keys until the room was empty, all having exited through the front doors. All respectable members were supposed to walk out the front door, which was generally a set of double doors propped wide open for exit. An anxious congregant could slip sideways out the other double door as the preacher was preoccupied with another member, and this was done.

The courtesy was that the congregants had to walk past the preacher, who was shaking hands, at the inside of the front doors. Though trite as this may sound, the handshake has vanished in the mega churches of today due to size. Later, Covid killed off the handshake even in smaller churches due to fear of death. Certainly, the holy kiss never traversed the centuries and the handshake appears to join in the loss.

The overhead projector was sensational until Power Point was discovered. With the projector, any wall or surface would bear charts, graphs, and the entire lesson if needed. The problem was applying the plastic sheet in a correct direction on the projector surface. This was done down the aisle twenty-five feet from the speaker. Many lessons were started with upside down tables and graphs and illegible print. It came to be a distraction more than a help and preachers grew tired of leaving the pulpit to fix the projector. It disappeared into oblivion shortly.

Power point followed and then the fast-paced visuals that have evolved today in the message. The internet has provided excellent back ground for so many lessons and sermons of today. If power goes out, the preacher is left to struggle.

The sound of Bible pages being turned in the sanctuary were a common noise, until the advent of the Bible app, and complete silence. In one congregation, of a thousand members, the sound of the pages turning were sharp and pronounced enough that the preacher made a comment. Now that sound is silent, as the scripture turns unheard within the electronics of the phone.

DANCING AND CAROUSING

The beautiful spring, with its warming of the temperatures and blooming of the flowers, brought another custom. It was pushed into the pulpit and found its way into a plethora of sermons. The sound was delivered with proper cadence, depth, and warnings. "This gathering should be avoided," the preacher droned on. He hit the high points of sin, debauchery and what he called "looseness" of the promenades, the junior-senior proms. Some of the high school dances, such as Homecoming and sock hops were thrown into the mix. A sock hop was criticized, by one preacher, as an event where a portion of clothes, the shoes, were removed at the beginning, setting the stage for the entire evening of seduction. Mindless circling of the Dairy Queen was mentioned.

Alcohol was, of course, the underlying concern. "It was a slippery slope." he maintained. Sleeping late and missing the services a day later was assumed to be a part of the whole sinful package. It was not "prom," it was "porn", one speaker opined. Another claimed that he had information that several prominent church-going mothers had gone to the store on the square, this week, looking for provocative dressings for their maidens to wear to the event. "Unbelievable," he chastised. "Debauchery in our midst."

Different religious groups had varied response to the events. Modern Baptists, Methodists and Presbyterians seemed to put forth the least resistance. Perhaps, they were more trusting of their youth. They were thoughtful, as they spearheaded a committee, to gain support of the parents and in turn have an event for their children that was peaceful and healthy. The Catholics offered no obstacle to the gathering.

Churches of the "hard shell "persuasion, and some of the smaller churches in the county, offered commentary that was critical of the event. One energetic preacher placed handbills in the pews condemning the gathering weeks prior. When the congregation reached for their Broadman Hymnals, a list of evils associated with dancing were visualized. As with most sins, opinions were unique to one and generally uncondemning to others. For some, the facts were that dancing was the culprit. Never mind that David danced partially clothed in the streets.

When wide eyed Ed Sullivan observed Elvis with his gyrating and movements, dancing was thrust out of the ballrooms and into the gymnasiums and youth centers of America. No one understood if the order of the inequity, was the dancing, or that alcohol might follow, or was it the glued closeness on the dance floor of these hormonal bodies? For some parents, it was a child growing up, that the parent wanted to delay, if possible. Many parents chaperoned the dances, and felt relieved when they found that Sodom and Gomorrah were not on full display. One preacher, and his wife, who were chaperones for the event, reported back to the congregation that all was well and no alcohol was spotted or smelled.

One of the more liberal groups, wondered if the "hard-shells" opposed sex because it could lead to dancing. It seemed that dancing was the worst of the sins. This movement in all directions, with spasms, whirling and twisting, as a band bellowed the music, was equated with all manner of ill behaviors. It was as if dancing was the root of all the Satanic problems in the world. Forget hunger, illicit sex, even damnation, it was dancing that caused Satan to spring into action. It was dancing that would be the downfall of America.

The opposition was common for a few brief decades, until so many real problems in society emerged, that this vice became the least of society's problems. Pointed sermons disappeared, the proms continued and the beautiful budding girls of youth were on display. This was to the delight of all the boys in the class. We could not keep our eyes off them, that was for sure, sinful or not.

I STARED AT HER SHOES

The driver motioned to the side of the road and said, "If you don't want to sit with her, you better clear that front seat." as he gestured toward the first row of seats in the school bus. Two students scattered off the front and headed to the back of the bus. He was blaring loudly as he looked upward at the students through a reflection in the mirror above him. I was staring at the driver. He stared at me. I met his eyes and looked down at my feet, breaking the stare. The world stopped and the bus went silent. All eyes were on the front door of the bus.

The driver slowed, the door squeaked and clambered opened, a lone black girl, standing in wet grass on the side of the road, she stepped up the two steps into the bus. She turned left, swinging slightly on the pole, propelling herself into the first seat right side, with moderate force. She immediately sat and looked forward out the clear glass window, as if in a daze. Her shoulders trembled ever so slightly. She then looked down at her shoes.

As I looked down at my shoes, I could see hers. I was two seats behind to her left. She was five feet from the driver. I noticed she had on a mildly tattered dress with leather strapped low heeled shoes that were worn. They were damp with dew. She stared downward. I stared at her shoes.

It was 1966, I was 13 and had an uncomfortable feeling. I knew what happened was wrong based on what we were taught at church. I did not understand it. I wanted to be somewhere else. I did not want to be here on this bus. I felt responsible, like I had made some big mistake, and I would get blamed. Like I had dropped and shattered some family heirloom with pieces and shards of China surrounding my feet. I had some sadness, but it did not stick. I had a brief minor thought that I should get up and go sit beside her. But I did not and could not. I was a weak, insecure, acne faced teenager already. I wanted no light shined on me. What I did not know, was that I was developing a conscience.

Kindness should be a reaction with an action. With no reaction, the bad action continues. Kindness should not be debated or scheduled by a committee. It should occur before laws force it to. Some kindness involves facing someone's mistreatment straight on full throttle. It could be us next time, a strange place among strange unkind people. Life has a way of following you around.

The rider never rode the bus again that I was aware of. She was not picked up nor was she standing on the side of the road. I looked daily when we topped that hill. Nobody. I realized I was party to an epic failure in my life- the lack of kindness to a neighbor. I knew it when it transpired and did nothing but hang my head, and stare at her shoes.

In 1970, it finally happened. The blacks from the segregated high school across town merged with whites at our high school. It was scheduled and planned. Adults wondered what would happen. Hushed conversations. There were no incidents. We were seniors that year, and concerned with the usual senior activities. We welcomed our classmates, who were also seniors. Our school class size doubled. We made lifelong friends; we sat in class together and ate together. Meals of fellowship. Our football team was much better with the merger. Life goes on. The Golden Rule was inching along on a journey, in our lives, powered by one smile at a time.

THE DAY THE SQUARE WENT SILENT

I held my mother's hand on the Square around 1962, as we watched an Impala Chevrolet, four doors, two occupants, meandering slowly, around the Courthouse. We were walking. It was slowing guardedly as it appeared to access the parking. The sounds of the lawn preacher were absent that day.

Preachers assembled on courthouse lawns throughout the South, 1940's, 50's, 60's. Sermons were preached as children hid and crouched in floorboards around the square. Some cried in their mama's arms on the lawn. A small crowd would gather. I would hide under the dashboard in the front seat of my daddy's 1960 Catalina Pontiac. I would raise slightly and catch glimpses of an apparent hollering madman, Bible in one hand, chopping motion like a hatchet in the other. The finger would jerk ceremoniously in a variation of a seizure, with a chop on every point. I could not avoid peering over the dashboard at this circus, eyes wide, blinking at the high points. I loved it. Very entertaining. When I grew taller than the dash, I quit watching and I assumed both I, and the preacher, had grown out of it.

The square also held political figures. A Governor, Gene Talmadge, a staunch segregationist, would scream that if elected, he would "remove all blacks from public office in Georgia." My grandfather, Adair Pinckney Chapman, heard him numerous times, in the 1930's and 40's. Gene would come into the county in a Cadillac, wearing a suit. Before entry to town, he would change into his overalls and ride in a borrowed truck conveying the image of the common man, here to serve the people.

I held my mama's hand. Her grip tightened. I looked and studied the car. In crisp, black, block letters on the door, it read, "Civil Rights Testing Car." I remember the car was white and the black letters jumped out in a startling fashion. Others stared from around the Square. My mother grasped my hand hard and took me to our car. Nothing was said.

I was blessed to live in a family not to hear others continually demeaned, because of social status in life or race. When we saw the destitute, my dad always said, "Be grateful and don't forget that you have had opportunities that others have not had."

My mother left the Square that day because of fear of violence, not perpetrated by the occupants of the car, but by others. The cars were sent to determine if equality of access was being denied in businesses, water fountains and other parts of life, because of color. It was a challenging of segregation and the separate but equal stance of the South. There were instances of strong and violent retaliation to these workers driving through the South. In the coming years, many died. The movie, "Mississippi Burning" told one of the stories. It was a sad period of violence and intolerance.

THE BURNING CROSS 1960

Several men in white robes, faces covered, hoisted the large cross into a hole. It went upright, and stood double their heights from the ground.

Earlier, an accelerant had been poured onto the wood. As soon as the cross was stable and pointed toward the heavens, others stepped back. One struck a match at the bottom of the structure. There was a brief flash and a fire ball shot upward like lightning and branched out to either side of the cross member as it traveled. The entire cross lit up and burned brightly in the night sky, flickering, and casting spooky shadows on hooded white uniforms standing silently. From the road through the window of a Ford, the eyeholes looked like black holes on the head of each white form.

We watched for a minute from our car, and my dad threw the Ford into gear as he said, "how crazy", sweeping the car sideways, into the other lane, to leave in a reverse direction. He exited at great speed, as if this embodiment of hate could be removed from the mind by acceleration in a Ford. The road was paved, the field was below us, down the embankment. We were gone in seconds.

My dad had shuffled us into the Ford that evening, with my mother, as twilight fell, explaining that he wanted to see if it was true. It was near a church where he had stood in the pulpit, so he knew the area in the county.

The mental picture of the fire pretty much blotted out whatever conversation remembrances there were from that night. If any other comments were made, they are not in my memory.

Fifty years later, I turned a corner in a Georgia community leaving a family reunion, and came upon 75 state patrol cars surrounding a downtown area. A large group was observing away from the barricades. I parked and learned that it was a Ku Klux Klan rally due in minutes. I asked my daughter, "did you want to see this?" advising her of my last experience as a child. Curiously, she said. "Yes." Grabbing her designer pocketbook and following me, we stood in an obvious protest group, hiding behind a tree to avoid a camera crew set up by the Atlanta press.

I heard a passerby ask the patrolman where the Klan was. The patrolman replied, "at Walmart." "Doing what?" the passerby said, "buying bedsheets and gasoline?" The patrolman said, "I hope not."

The dozen or so robe- covered participants entered from a square direction, waved their unlit cross around. It was considerably smaller than my remembrance from 1961. They were marching with banners flapping in the breeze, hoods, but faces uncovered, apparently because it is against the law otherwise. With a smaller cross, no fire and uncovered faces, I guess this was KKK Lite, 21st century. A speech from the spokesman ensued, asking for "Christian volunteers" as this was a "family organization."

A little boy, no more than six years of age stepped to the barricade and hollered, "You all are crazy." He returned to be with his parents. Several clapped in the crowd after his outburst. Hope for the world from a child. A lady in a wheelchair quietly passed out "love your neighbor" pamphlets.

We peeked from behind the oak tree, not wanting to be seen by anyone within fifty miles. They marched off as quickly as they had come, cross in hand. My daughter and I shook our heads in disbelief and left the security of the oak tree, dodging a camera man and leaping into our car.

I thought of the symbol, the cross. Jesus having died as God watched, on that cross, for all colors of skin. How could a representation be so misplaced?

THE HOME VISIT

T he road was a narrow mud hole with deep tracks where few cars had made the drive. It was like a thousand other roads in the south. It was on a rural route that was muddy in rain or dirt, in the sun. Until somebody's nephew or daddy or brother was elected to the county commission, it would probably stay unpaved. When it was paved, it was possible that the longest living settler would have it named after him. The naming of roads, like giving of flowers, happens after death.

We slid slightly sideways as we traversed, bumping large chrome handles inside the car as it leaned outward. You couldn't spin the tires or you would launch into the streams on either side, as if traveling between two moats. We avoided the ditch by inches. We turned into the yard, the rear of the Pontiac sliding sideways as we entered.

We did not park where she had raked the wet sandy area in front of the house with her little straw broom. Yard of the month, but no grass. A doctor was leaving the front porch as we approached, bound for his next appointment scattered in the county on some dirt road. Preachers and doctors did that back then. House Calls. They came to your home. A quaint artifact now from a bygone era. The doctor would check a blood pressure, look at the bottles surrounding the side table and make solemn recommendations to the sad family assembled like a death choir in the living room, diagonally along the side of the bed.

We passed a mangy dog at the porch scratching his head, cleaned muddy shoes at the front door, and stepped into the living room. The mantle of the fireplace held pictures of old people in faded overalls with spectacle glasses. One frame held a man captive in a suit ready to drive a mule driven wagon to go preach ten miles away on a Sunday morning- the dying woman's father from 1920.

The sick woman clung to life in a hospital bed set obliquely in the living room. It was the only room in the house large enough for the bed to be accessible on both sides, the bed was positioned diagonally. The location of the bed was common. Sickness moved you from the bedroom to the living room which became the dying room and then to the family plot miles away in the cemetery. In the cemetery, adjacent to the church where you had accepted Jesus and attended for 80 years. It was a predictable time. Birth, life, service to God for most, then death.

The woman stirred and said, "thanks for coming." Gratitude. People were always grateful in those times. Always thankful for what life they had, amidst, with some, much poverty and sickness.

It was a praying time. We prayed for rain to come, we prayed for rain to go. We prayed for the sick confined to a bed in their living room on a long muddy dirt road. A standard prayer was for those of the "household of faith." We prayed to live, we prayed for God to take us. We prayed for the preacher that was asked to leave, we prayed for the replacement. We prayed for crops to flourish, we prayed for weeds to fall by the wayside. We prayed for our unborn children in the womb, we prayed for our children at school. We prayed for the president of the nation, we prayed for the president of the PTA. We prayed for the rich. We prayed for the poor. Every angle of life, both good and bad was bathed in prayer, by somebody somewhere, every day. The future was marching us forward.

THE WAKE

The open casket sat in the front room out from the fireplace. The living room where he was no longer living. A paradox. The viewing was in full swing. The man, in peaceful repose, hands folded in eternal rest, had passed from this life. The hands were stained by the hot sun, dark, shrunk and discolored, a mature farmer for 50 years. Hands that would work no more. They resembled having passed across the river Jordan a long time ago. I wondered if part of him had died before another. I guessed one could live if the part was something that could be spared, like a gall bladder, tonsils or a spleen, maybe hands. We knew a boy who had lost a spleen and he did well. I surmised if the heart died, the rest would follow in short order. To complete the picture, all the heart had to do was stop beating.

It was summer, the fireplace was cold. The house was arranged with the front living room leading out onto the porch. It was a small home, four or five rooms, a little bigger than a "shot gun" house, where one could see from the front door straight out the back door. The well for drinking water was always on the back porch, the kitchen was at the back. The larger gatherings of people were at the back. Most people can only sit so long with a deceased person adjacent to them, as small talk is made about the natural appearance of the corpse. My grandmother said, "she never knew a dead person who looked natural." The remarks were made and the visitation adjourned as far from the casket as possible, to the back of the house. Food was a welcome respite from the living room and the body.

"I wonder if he has on shoes," My brother said. We had been left in the front room on a sofa, our feet not touching the floor, with instructions to behave. I was intrigued by the thought of shoes on a dead man. I knew funerals were expensive, caskets cost money, clothes were given by the family to the mortician, if not, the undertaker, as we called him, provided them – for a fee. Mortician clothes had no pockets. I had been amazed when the preacher told me that and had proceeded to check out every corpse's attire. When asked why this one had pockets, I was told that the family provided the attire.

I said, "look and see if he has on shoes." I never expected him to honor that request. To my astonishment, my brother, barely 7 years old, leaped to the mid portion of the casket and poked his head down while gently pawing the curtain at the midsection, allowing him to peer down into the dark corridor on the lower half of the body. "Nope," he said. "Socks only, the ones we don't like."

This disturbed me greatly. I felt the family had been both short changed and invalidated. I decided that any reputable person should be buried in shoes. If not shoes, then just put us dead in the casket in pajamas. We wore clothes with shoes, we should die in clothes with shoes, our best shoes- Sunday go to "meeting" shoes. We're going into the afterlife practically barefooted. Preposterous. A sacrilege.

It made no sense to me, but that concern quickly dissipated when I realized my younger brother had one upped me to the maximum. I had been dethroned from my first-born status. I wanted to cheat Esau like Jacob did. He had touched a casket, even better, the inner lining. We were certainly used to death. With our father, the preacher, we could have conducted funerals ourselves by the time we were ten years old. We sat in grieving groups with the open casket in the middle, hours at a time. We were accustomed to tears and stricken folks and all the conversation. We were used to hearing stories of the end, how the patient got there, and all the particulars. But this, touching the casket interior, this was way out there. Retribution from parents would have been hard and quick.

I had read Tom Sawyer and often envied his juvenile delinquent state. This was my moment. I knew what I had to do. I searched and found a pen. The only paper I had was a Juicy Fruit gum wrapper. On the blank inside, block print, readable, I carefully printed, "let me out, I'm not dead." This I read aloud for effect to my brother's wide eyes. With a sweeping motion and bravery of war, I slung the curtain aside like a matador in the bull ring. I thrusted the paper and as it wafted in the stirring air, it landed delicately on a dead knee. I then stared at my aghast brother and said, "top that one." I resumed my seat, confident that I had done the ultimate in sibling superiority.

By then, we had been alone with the corpse the allotted time that God would allow. The room suddenly filled with entrants from both the front porch and the kitchen. There was no way I could remove the note, nor had I thought this act of rebellion out. I was doomed. Petrified with fear, my mother and father hustled us out, anxious to get home as it was late. I mouthed the words to my brother on the steps, "If you tell mama, I will kill you." Emphasis on "kill". The threat worked; he kept quiet.

Then the nail-biting worries began. How fast could they get this man buried without finding my note? I came in from school the next day. "Have they buried the man yet, "I asked. "No" Mama said, "they are waiting on family from out west." Oh, God help me. I repent. I knew my days were numbered. Would it be found? Would I be jailed at the juvenile farm? What possessed me to do that? I didn't realize that I would ask that question a few more times in my life. I told God that I was yet grown, thinking of only immediate gratification. "Yes, I said, I am a delinquent."

The days passed just like the man had and he and the periodical were planted in the cemetery. No mention of a note. God spared me a discipline. The tomb was sealed, the note safe.

I wondered if he were exhumed for some reason and the note found, would the family decide that he had been buried alive? I knew that result was impossible because there was no pen in the coffin. Hence, no handwritten note in the dark. Tom Sawyer would have slipped the pen in his hand. I just know he would have. Perhaps this was a failure on my part.

THE LONGEVITY OF THE BURIAL PROCESS

S egregation has lasted long and hard in the business of death. At this traumatic time, one might postulate that death was too private, too deeply personal, to allow for any disruption or integration of the races. Neither side has protested to enter funeral homes or beauty parlors. Barbershops and funeral homes were generally segregated. It was a walled off area, where no racism was seen or heard. The blacks and whites were allowed to have funerals in peace, though they were not generally buried in the same cemetery. Both used adorned floral caskets, and marched from the church to the cemetery with a procession of friends and family. The blacks and whites mourned, often together, showing love for each other.

A funeral was a reminder that we are all in the human race, it's us against the world. Eventual death is the hallmark of the world. We are all terminal.

Certainly, there were instances of integrated funerals, the black or white pillars of the community and many others had integrated support for their final hour. Primarily, as far as embalming and handling the service, the funeral homes were generally segregated and apart for the races. The manner of the funerals was somewhat different. The corpse was still dead and there were mourners, but the production of the funeral was different. The black process was typically longer, up to a week of mourning before planting the body in the ground. The individual reading of the flower cards at the service took a while and was done at the funeral. One after the other, the funeral director held the card high and announced the sender. Amens and vocal support filled the air.

Cremation for either race was rare. It was sometimes preached in both churches, black and white. "God is the only one who has the power to burn you up." As the price of funerals came to equal that of an automobile, the pulpit restriction came to be lifted and the less expensive cremations thrived. The Pope authorized the Catholics to have cremation as a choice in 1963. It was 20 years before it became fashionable in other churches.

In truth, a cremation simply increased the degrading of the mortal body in a faster manner, than it was going to accrue at the normal rate of tissue decomposition. There was no indication of a scriptural prohibition on that manner of burial. But there's an emotional aspect of any church question.

Complaints heard about cremation generally were fear by the parents of busy children losing the urn, selling mistakenly as a vase in a garage sale, storing it in the smokehouse, or forgetting it at the funeral home. This was solved with burial of the urn at the cemetery or above ground vaults. The idea of the public not being able to see grandma for closure was a consideration. Psychologists for years had maintained that the viewing of the body in a service assisted in the grief process. This was all cussed, discussed, mangled and spit out, but the burden of funeral expense quenched the deal with some in the 1970's and today.

A widow called the preacher and asked "where he put the urn at the funeral." The preacher, shocked, said, "I never had it." The preacher called the funeral home and asked the location of the urn. The funeral director hesitated, and said, "Come on by, I will have one for you." The preacher picked it up and asked no questions.

The unusual aspect of injuries and dying in the South in 1963 was the absence of 911 or any emergency vehicles. There was no race to the Emergency Room with sirens flashing. When an auto accident occurred, the authorities notified the funeral homes, which were gracious enough to transport the sick and injured to the hospital. It was undetermined as to which home was given the spoils of accidents.

Minding my own business driving through a neighborhood, I was broad sided by another big chrome car, which ejected me out my passenger door into a lady 's yard. A most disturbed family called the police and shortly a long black hearse rounded the corner, slow and methodical, like they always drive. The hearse eased up. With my father performing funerals, I was familiar with the model.

The people that caused the wreck piled out of their car screaming about a broken thumb and cursing me, the 16-year-old, for my reckless endangerment. They proudly told the funeral director that I was the culprit. Because they screamed first, they were placed in in the hearse first, the wide sideways doors flaring open. The caloric challenged lady on a gurney sprawled out screaming about her broken thumb. She was installed first, while her children cried. I was relegated with my slashed bleeding head to a box beside her in the back of the hearse, leaning against the side, where I dripped blood on the floor. There were several of us, packed in there like sardines, but I had the small box seat to myself.

A ride in a hearse is a big beast of a machine with dips in the road and the gliding along resembling a local fair ride. It takes an acre to turn a hearse around and as the undertaker made the broad arc sweep into the hospital emergency area, my stomach tickled like the rollercoaster we rode yearly. The arc completed, the hearse was backed in promptly and the rear door opened. Thoughts of being loaded back up and carried away was on all our minds. The silence grew, as we realized we were being prepared for reentry. The wide back door was left open, ominously.

With the door open, I leaped out and ran into the emergency room, facing a doctor who could hear the lady yelling," he broke my thumb." The doctor scowled at me and said, son," what did you do?" I told him that the screamer had indeed run the stop sign and that I was innocent. My appearance, one side of my head bloody, long black hair and a ripped army jacket from a Goodwill store appeared to solidify my guilt and I received no sympathy. I walked out later, sutures in my head, a brace on multiple fractured ribs, past the open rear door of the hearse, as I stiffened. I was exonerated by the judge a week later and the screamer with arm in cast was fined 10 dollars for running a stop sign. I sat smug as the judge lectured her. I was vindicated at last.

In the funeral period, limousines were used in both races to carry the family, one last effort at death, to show the world, that this person deserved a slow splendid ride to the cemetery. The skinny undertaker, head peering over the wide steering wheel, drove and waxed in the experience.

The southern funeral had many moving components, there was the death and the transport to the funeral home, the attire of the participants and the deceased, the obituary, the mourning and the menu. The menu involved two moving parts, one as to what food was carried to the home, and another as to what was served at the church after the service. Different church members would be in charge of each.

The food that would come into play would dwarf the fellowship meals that churches offered to preachers. The mourning process could only be maintained with stamina, strength, and lots of calories. There were cakes, pies, vegetables, and all the food groups. They were piled high in the back bedrooms and kitchens of the deceased. It was as if the sadness could be ameliorated with caloric consumption. A steady stream of women bringing casserole dishes and pots and pans were seen. Both southern blacks and whites knew how to eat. It has been our hallmark.

After the funeral period, the containers would be placed clean and dried on a bed, calls would go out that the dishes are ready to be picked up. That was the husband's job, to return to the home of the deceased and pick up the containers left by their wives.

The story goes that a teacher asked a class to bring to school an item from their family typifying their faith. One first grader brought a crucifix, another the bible. A Baptist brought a casserole dish. Both these items had intense spiritual significance in each faith, it appeared.

The mourning process was long and emotional, taxing the strength of all the church members. The climatic event was of course the funeral, but the visitation, with body at hand, was significant. This visitation was at the home of the deceased until it drifted to the church in the 1970's. The mourners would hug the family, comment on the beauty of the corpse, the simplicity of the coffin and any other part that could be conceived as providing comfort and security of the family. In tragic unexpected death situations, some wanted to be as near the mourning as possible. This would involve hours in line and congregated groups in the foyer. Some wanted to become part of the event.

The church visitation, the evening before the funeral, was a heavy affair. After viewing the deceased with appropriate comment, the mourners would turn around and plop down in one of the many pews in the church. It was not unusual for half the church to fill up before the visitation was over. The widow collapsed many times and sat on the front row.

As preacher's kids we would play down behind the pews observing rear view of the backs of all the feet facing forward in the church. The men, many farmers, wore socks that would not stay up. My brother and I despised that sock with no elastic, at the top, as well as the white color that so many had. Most wore Sunday best to the visitation, though it was not the funeral. That happened the next day.

The attire for the funeral was Sunday best, dark suits on the men and black dresses on the women. The woman put a lot of thought into what to wear at funerals, from gloves to hose. A mistake could cast a bad light on an entire family as a sign of disrespect. The deceased could wear his favorite suit, which had pockets. The ones sold by the funeral home had no compartments for the final eternal journey.

The family was told in 1949 that the preacher was

dying at Crawford Long Hospital in Atlanta. The end was near and the doctors pronounced him quickly terminal. The abdomen was full of poison and sepsis. A funeral was eminent and the mother-in-law had no appropriate new dress. She immediately bought the whole outfit, gloves, shoes and dress. The father, with much prayer rallied, the funeral was cancelled and he lived 47 more years. The cousins in the family told and retold the story of the sweet, kind, gentle grandmother deciding prayers were done and purchasing a funeral dress for a living man. Sometimes in the midst of tragedy, it is easy to give up on God. But God has other plans that we don't know about.

Some folks seemed to thrive on funerals, to pull forth and bear up under many of the parts, seemingly enjoying their proximity to the whole affair. Any public office holder needed to have a visible appearance, well seen and well heard in the home of the deceased, the visitation, and certainly the funeral. Though the corpse would not be doing future voting, except in some instances, there were living votes at hand that would be cast in the next election. Many politicians had lost at the polls for absence from funerals and weddings. The absence was detected by the family of the deceased but also by those in attendance who also observed what families were represented. Representation by a visiting member of the family was not as good as attendance by multiple family members, but did show concern.

Lastly, came the ride from the church to the cemetery, slow and methodical, led by the hearse with the enclosed body, family, and mourners. All cars had their lights on and rolled as close as possible through town on traveled routes, generally eager to be seen by the masses. Any respectable southerner who met the procession would pull off, remove his hat, and sit respectfully on the road shoulder until the entire entourage traveled by. You would note that the ones that did not pull over and whizzed on by, facing or passing the procession had out of state tags. Usually northern. The procession would roll into the cemetery, right up to the gravestones, as close as possible to the grave. Family would then embark across the graves to the tent. Children would disregard any admonitions from the adults and dance across as many tombstones as possible, before reprimands were given.

Then, there was the graveside service, many times under a hot Georgia sun with a small tent for the closest mourners. The grave was dug by equipment or by hand, a tent was erected, and a turf like material was placed around the grave in sheets to appear less threatening and muddy. No one wanted to see raw dirt adjacent to a coffin. It would have been too much of a reminder as to what was transpiring there.

This area, a foot or more, from the entry to the grave on all sides, was unsteady and not safe for walking or full weightbearing. The preacher giving the eulogy had to be careful. There was a distance that was too close to the grave to be supported. The material hid the clogs and uneven surfaces and the mud, but was highly unstable.

In one funeral, an eight-year-old, holding the hand of her grandfather, as he did the eulogy, suddenly loss footing. She was peering into the hole, trying to see as much of the casket as possible, her feet slipped and dropped a foot into the grave. She tumbled, saved only by the hand of the grandfather that she was holding, who jerked her back onto solid ground. She was shaken, but did not cry, and the matter was over in seconds, the grandfather never missing a beat, continuing his praise for the deceased, quoting scripture without stopping.

One family, desiring to cast a last glance at the deceased, demanded the casket be opened again, right there in the cemetery, in the sweat and stifling heat. The sun beating was down as if to punish the participants. The undertaker addressed his helpers, "open her up boys, open her up" and they did. The last quick good bye was given and the ceremony completed. The family was then at peace and the funeral was over.

As mourners left the southern cemetery, they were drawn to the many graves they traversed, noting the epitaphs and sayings. "I told you I was sick" was one, another, "sleep on sweet babe and take thy rest, God called thee home, he thought it best." This sparked conversations about all the deceased folks from the area. This occupied several minutes. There was always a soldier's grave that was spotted and several would respectfully stand and commensurate over his life. This was 1960's. We loved our country and the men and women that fought for it. The cemetery was a healing of sorts, for the mourners in the community, at each funeral.

One son, who had driven all night from Texas, accompanied is father, the preacher, to the funeral. The son was also a minister. His father had the service, both graveside and church. As the son stood beside his father, before the graveside service began, his tired mind wandered to another thought. He leaned quietly over and asked his father where the deceased would be buried. His father, looking incredulous, said, "there" pointing five feet to the visible casket and grave. The exhausted son gulped, and said nothing.

The same overworked preacher got up at a 6:00 PM

wedding and said, his mind on a 2:00 funeral, "This is a sad occasion." When this dissolved into his mind, he quickly recovered. "For the parents of the bride who are losing a daughter, but are gaining a wonderful son in law." The guffaw appeared to have been handled. He could last another day.

JESUS AND THE CERAMIC PIG

T he multi- colored pig was spied as my brother and I sat on the sofa. It sat solemnly on the mantle, brightly painted ceramic, like the ones you would see sold at fruit stands in towns like Bascom, Two Egg or Alford, Florida on the way to Panama City Beach. The home was a small humble abode, the head of household was a frail widow who had missed the services the last two weeks. The preacher and his family had come to visit and pray for this little, kind, sick member. We were cramped into a little room in an uninsulated shot gun house with a cool breeze blowing in and around the windows, despite the old gas heater, attempting to heat the universe.

It was hot, stuffy, and I wanted mobility. Movement is key with a ten-year-old. I inched my way to the mantle in a non- chalant manner. I maneuvered a spot behind the tiny form in the rocking chair. Her little stories of her family travails were told to the sympathetic ear of the preacher. Low voiced discussions were heard. It was a struggle of poverty against the world. I stood on the hearth, gathered my thoughts, and reached for the mantle pig. What a beauty. I stood on tip toes with visions of the frail woman presenting me with the pig for showing up with my parents today. Surely my presence was good for something. This might be it.

I put one hand on each side of the pig and lifted, then turning it 45 degrees to position it and remove it sideways, above the gray-haired head and across the mantle. Alas, it was not to be. At the Isaac Newton appropriated time, gravity separated the two parts of the pig. The pig was engineered in a manner different than I had contemplated. I was left with the body of the pig in my hands, while the head dropped like a boulder upon the slightly bald head of the elderly Christian. When it hit her head, it popped into two pieces, as probably each pig had done that sold in the State of Florida at some point in their traumatic lives.

A shriek, then a muffled scream pierced the air of the home visit. She winced with pain and shook her head as a baseball player does who is struck on the mound. She regained composure, one hand on her head as she attempted to turn and determine what in the world I had done. She realized the pig was now disjointed and lying on the hearth. She looked down at the pig, still holding the top of her head and then looked at me. Her face was so wrinkled that pain could not be diagnosed; no gauge could be measured to determine if real damage had occurred.

The visitation was quickly adjourned. It was found that a large goose egg laid atop her head, but no blood. A fully self-contained head hematoma. She could not see it, thank God. The ashen faces of my parents and brother told the story, as we leaped into the car, leaving the woman with her pig in three pieces. She had spread them out on the kitchen table as we picked them up off the hearth. Sometimes in life, there's nothing to do but leave.

When the car doors closed, I was afraid that I could be mercilessly back handed from the front seat, but that was not the verdict. My dad could not control his pent -up laughter, it burst forth in the car as we pulled out of the muddy driveway. He shook his head and did not speak one word to me, as my mother said, "Can you believe that happened?"

There was retribution. I was seated and advised to write a letter of apology explaining my juvenile, delinquent actions and asking for forgiveness. She accepted, or so she said at church, with a smile occupying most of her face. She resumed her seat on her pew and the matter was laid to rest. But I never forgot my dad's paroxysmal outburst in the car post event. I had some satisfaction with having made him laugh, though at her expense.

A FATHER'S POIGNANT PRAYER

The phone rang late, with a ring that spelled distress. The sound in a house with wood floors bounced off the walls like a clanging cymbal. Very disturbing. The telephones had ringers then, no soft tones. There were real bells with large noises. There's an aura of uncertainty with the sound in blackness of a telephone after bedtime echoing through a dark house. Or at least it was then. Phone calls were less then. There were no telemarketers. It was common to hear, "wonder who's dead" before the phone was answered. Late night phone calls carried bad news. This time it was again accurate. A son had died in Texas, states away from his father in Georgia. The father had notified a few church members and requested they come to the building. God always seemed closer in the building. True, it wasn't a tabernacle where God's presence was known to reside, but it was a place of prayer a few days a week with joy and tears from the congregation. They knew God was there and felt closer to him there. There was a connection.

The late-night calls went out, I was a passenger with my dad enroute to the tragic meeting. They met on the first two rows of the church building. It was like an invitation to the altar. with a couple of full church pews occupied at the end of the song. The mourner's bench, as some called it, the process of going forward in the church building with conviction of faults.

They met in a group, they hugged, they cried. The death of a son. One man said, "Nobody should have to bury a child", as if it should be a national law. I did not know exactly what it meant, as I had never had a child. I was a child. But I had heard that before in the tragedies that I had traversed with my dad. I heard it again that night. It took years and births before I knew what it meant.

That night the men gathered initially at the front of the building. Then one said, "let's pray". I was a kid, but the men were brothers, brothers in Christ and so duly called. The father of the deceased son indicated that he would begin. I was puzzled by this. I thought the men had come to pray for him. We sat down in the first two pews on the left side of the building. The grieving father sat and slid from the pew to the floor and knelt. His head closer to the floor than the rest of him, almost touching the floor. I watched and waited with curiosity of a child. What would he say? What could he say? What does this mean? He was the bereaved, the victim, yet he was praying.

He then prayed to God. It was not a steady level voice. There was a break or two in the sentence. But he was firm and coherent. He wept. He asked for guidance and help in this time of trial. He praised God for blessings, I remember that. It was a poignant prayer, noted by myself, even at my young age. I was developing empathy at a very young age for seeing this kind of faith in someone, in an hour of severe distraught tragedy. I understood it and marveled at its years later.

I remember thinking later, backwards, that this man prayed so deeply and so boldly that it was a curiosity to me. It is etched in memory. Was it faith or foolishness? I saw it and wondered if I could have that same thing, whatever it was and how he could have that attitude in a future that was so uncertain, and in a world that I had learned could be a horrible place. A world the exact opposite of the way Sunday School described heaven. I wondered that night if God somehow came down and installed some invisible shield around the man to protect him from this event. He seemed inoculated against the hopeless tragedy. His faith was monumental. His system was fully mature. I knew he would survive. He encouraged the people that had come to encourage him.

Nights like this started with the night call, the slamming of car doors, the fast ride down dirt roads or blacktops, the pulling up to the church or a home, the prayers, the kneeling, the weeping, and the consoling of the bereaved, and finally, the knock at the door and in some cases, the funeral director leaving with the body. I was shaken by the suddenness of tragedy and death, the leap it could make into a serene, casual and unconcerned life. I was stable in mind, learning about a faith that seemed elusive but discoverable. There were the home visits with the tattered, the shattered and broken, the orphans and the faithful. I was learning to handle and compartmentalize the experiences, to shut out some of the sadness and grief that I was being exposed to. But then, the child drowned.

ABSALOM, MY SON, MY SON

As I tried to keep up, my father walked briskly. He was walking, I was running. We entered the funeral home and went down a corridor to a small room, full of men. Within seconds, the mournful words I heard down the hall, from the room, were clear and understandable. The sobs of one father swathed the air, one side of the sky to the other, voice rising and falling. Cadence. A wet rag swabbing a dying universe. "Please God, bring him back so I can tell him I love him one more time." This went out across the small crowd and bounced around the room, before it faded away. It then started again. The little boy was supine on the table in the funeral home. The father laid down obliquely across the motionless body of his son, having been transported in. The sides of the diaper bulged with water and buoyancy, but not enough to have held the child up in the water. It could not save him. Moist skin was mildly blue. The father assuming the most reverent stature, bowing and kneeling at the same moment, lying across his fallen son, begging God to raise his son.

I thought of my grandfather who went to his knees behind the pew every time a prayer was uttered. I wondered if I should now as well, but dismissed the thought, I wasn't big enough. Kneeling was for big people. Then I remembered Timmy, on the television show, "Lassie", who knelt every night beside his bed with bedtime prayers. I stood anxiously, my eyes never leaving the body.

I expected the child to rise up and go home with his father. It sounded like a reasonable request to me. I was 11 years old. I knew the flannel board at church had few problems. There were frayed edges and sometimes Ruth did not stick beside Naomi, but overall, it laid out life in a tidy form. There were the Seven Days of Creation, The Mosaic Age, the Ten Plagues, The Christian Age and most all biblical events. I couldn't get Peter to appear realistic on the shore. He was not positioned far enough away from Jesus on the Sea of Galilee. There was not enough flannel. But tonight, this was off the flannel board in another land. Far away. Foreign. A place of ragged, frayed flannel and unanswered questions. It was somewhere I had never visited, never begged to go. But there I was, the only young child in the room a few feet from the boy.

I stood waist high, in front of my father's suit pants and the denim of many men. The salt of the earth, God fearing men of the community were there. The call went out and the men poured in. A sea of support present with giant opposition to this tragedy, to be reckoned with by the community and God.

There were a few sobs, much shock and ashen faces. It was as if they were frozen and I was the only one that could move. I heard nothing but the father and the sound of my breathing. I moved closer to the little boy. He had no tears, only stillness. Get up, I thought. Go home. God get him up. I thought of Lazarus on the flannel board, stumbling out of the tomb with bandages, pinched between my thumb and forefinger. Bandages were peeled off and he was as good as new, gone with Martha and Mary back to his home. It was a simple answer for a prayer, just get up and go home. A simple request. Take me home. It's what we all want for a lifetime.

My dad had received the call and I had bolted into our car and rode into town. My mother stayed home with my younger brother. After the incident, we rode home in silence. After my dad's death in 1996, I realized we had not had a conversation about it throughout the last thirty-five years.

Fifty- five years after the event, a diary surfaced given to my friend by his sister, having described the death in her diary, written when she was 16. She documented visiting that night with her mother at the house of the tragedy. The wails, sobs and grief had been transcribed in the diary, and still remembered, vividly by the writer, 55 years later.

Driving beside the home, a passerby heard the father loudly calling and searching for the child. Upon his return in minutes, he observed the father holding the child in his arms walking back to the house, having been found in a body of water, a pond, a short distance away.

As I changed diapers on my children and grandchildren throughout the years, the bulging sides of the diaper would trigger a sudden forceful memory and, in a flash, or some smaller degree of eternal measurement, I was thrown back into that room. Standing still. Nobody is moving. I hear the father pray the mournful request to God, again. A branding iron was passed into my cortex that night, indelibly printing it. I watch. I wait, still expecting even now a miracle, maybe it's a dream. In a blink, the scene vanishes, gone like a setting sun, glimpsed briefly at the juncture of ocean and sky, before disappearing below the surface.

I'm locked back into the present, facing a smiling child in a new diaper, eyes shining up at me like the stars in Abraham's sky. He looks up at me, as I say, "I love you." I grip and squeeze and hold him hard enough to never let him go and vow to never let him leave my sight. I realize again, immediately, that is impossible. Children and grandchildren have to leave, they must live and grow and discover and feel and experience love and distress. They must see life and sadness and goodness and all the things that there are to see. Things we have seen. Things we don't want them to see. I know they must pass that way as well. Mistakes made. Regrets given. Misdirected actions, Lost opportunities. I sense total defeat and my mind leaves the tension and the child and goes to the Sovereignty of God, where it has gone for so many decades. I think hard, one more time, perhaps the thousandth time. I see Jesus on a cross depicted in blessed sermons of youth. The visual is clear. He's dying to be raised. A father above flips the cosmic switch and darkens the sky. In that dim light, in the crowd, standing near the cross is Mary. Looking up, she sees her own dying son. I briefly wonder, if she had a thought, "Please bring him back so I can tell him I love him, one more time."

Is this what following Jesus is? Is it at a point of horror, bold despair, slumped in a heap in front of neighbors, over the lifeless body of a beloved son, helpless, broken by the world, caring not what others may think? Is this when the Spirit of God is the closest to our very soul, engaging us, holding us, comforting us with groans too deep for words?

THE SOVEREIGNTY OF GOD

There is a vague longing for order and schedule in our lives, until we recognize it, become bored with it and cast it aside. It seems to start with regular feedings of the baby, then degenerates into eating much while hungry at various times. Sometimes, we are our own villainous architects, assembling our lives into a most dreadful set of circumstances, many times caused by our own immaturity and failure to address known problems. Other times, we are innocent bystanders, victims of life, which has become disorderly and disorganized without our impute. The tragedies are sudden and brutal. Bones splinter in all directions, cancer metastasizes like tentacles throughout the body. Hearts stop. Lungs rest. The rent comes due. The car motor blows up. A trauma, then another, striking with an unrelenting abuse and turning our world upside down. Some are more harmed than others, backs broken along with the heart. The good die young.

In Chicago, my neuroanatomy teacher, a small man

with an appearance as if the weight of the world was upon shoulders, said, with a plump, solemn face, of gliomas, "and nature can be so cruel as to give this tumor to a child.", gesturing toward the many creases and folds in the brain on the screen. He rolled "cruel" off his tongue with an elongated dialect, a way to stretch his surprise at nature or maybe his unbelief in God. I did not know. I speculated that he had seen so much trauma that it left him stunned and without belief, but I could not be sure. I thought of our nineth grade classmate years earlier, who died of a brain tumor, and a brief shade of sadness passed before me and then dissipated.

A childhood friend's father dies, the son is taken by his brother for a ride around in the family car for hours to calm one another. I thought about riding in a car knowing my daddy was gone. I couldn't comprehend it. The wheels turned that night, but never arrived at a destination. The rhythmic hum of the car seemed to calm the grief-stricken son and they returned home in the wee hours, but daddy wasn't there.

Within all this, from joy to calamity, we live our lives with an opinion and an option, of the Sovereignty of God. To some it's a distant thought, to others, it arrives every day in the midst of tragedies, "Where is God? "One will ask?", peering into a casket.

A distraught, grown son, face grimaced, eyes flooded, and fists tightly clinched, pounded on the emergency room glass asking God, why? His elderly mother lay dead on a gurney, she was stabbed at least thirty times. I was one of the crew in the emergency room that treated the patient. I was supposed to do something. I had provided a saphenous vein cut down on the lower leg, a feeble attempt to provide an intravenous lifesaving volume of fluid. It was inserted in seconds, the fluids ran into the dying woman, her organs so damaged and punctured that life ebbed away, regardless of the measures to save it. She was the victim of a home invasion. Alone, she stood no chance. As her son struck the glass, it bowed, but did not shatter. I sensed that it needed to. I wanted it to break wide open in a million parts and clatter to the ground. Let the universe give a crashing sound to his grief, some affirmation that he had a right to be stricken with grief. However, almost miraculously, it did not break.

His tears made the glass foggy and slick. Two fists pounded, as if he were locked out. He collapsed against the glass and slid to the pavement beneath it. He then pulled himself up, and walked away into the dark parking lot, leaving the body of this mother behind. His shoulders slumped, sobbing with pure unadulterated grief gripping him like a vise, having come face to face with the evil of the world. The Sovereignty of God, what does it mean?

In the first printed book by Gutenberg, and also having become the most printed, it is found. The Sovereignty of God, which leaps from every page and paragraph. Sovereignty was already there, but was made known to us in the beginning of all things and time. The beginning before other beginnings. The first proclamation, "In the Beginning, God." No proof is provided. The Word is just thrown out there in its simplicity. The most controversial statement ever written. Unbelievers curse, scream, tear clothes and march in the streets demanding proof. Alternately, believers weep when they consider the image that they share with the Creator and the grace that sustains us in this horrible fallen world.

In the natural, we cannot conceive of a beginning from nothing, but there it is, "ex nihilo", something from nothing. We know we confront the God of the Bible, in the beginning. According to Paul and John, we stumble upon Jesus as well. The universe was formless, shapeless, empty and dark over the surface. The beginning of our history was a dark, scary place. The Holy Spirit is hovering over the surface. We can imagine it, in the dark, if we close our eyes quietly contemplating our existence. Change is coming. And then, from nowhere and yet everywhere, God speaks. The Divine Imperative. The most important verbal sounds ever uttered since that moment in history. God, who is infinite and has been here since before time is moving and he's commanding. "Let there be light,", the first words spoken to a dark place, unformed and void. It is as if a cosmic switch is flipped and light covers the universe, all things are visible, all of the chaos and void and nothing are bathed in light, pure bright, the light of Yahweh. Had we been there, we could not have seen the source and lived. When we leave this earth eternally, believers will be bathed in it.

Created over a few days, the sixth day brings a man, as God, who created the world by command, actually bends down and molds a man out of dust and breathes deep into the lungs. Breath and life. A creature, but made in God's image. Not omnipotent or omnipresent like God, but able to have a will, and emotion, and able to worship the God who created him. It was all good, except something was not good. Man was lonely. A helper was made for Adam, her name would be Eve. God rested on the seventh day. Mankind as a couple was created and capped off a week of preparation of the world and mankind entered on the seventh day having been made by the hands of God. As God rested that day, they lived. And then it was good.

In the first few words of the Bible, we learn that we did not rise out of slime, unwanted and precariously made, on that day. We are not children of some point of origin or big blast from a godless universe that formed us into model citizens that could live and breathe. If we were, we would have no destiny and no purpose. Life would have as much meaning as a rock or a plant, a bird or a bee, a cornstalk or a displaced mountain. We are not cosmic aberrations with no future. There is more in front of me than I can see, God can visualize much better than I can dream. Our horizons are stretched into an eternity. We were known before we were born. We were known in the womb by God in quite a big way, like the ways we are knitted together. Our hair is numbered, our soul's eternal, our destiny extends forward. Redemption is coming.

Our days on earth have been plotted and mapped according to Paul in Acts 17. Nothing has been left to chance, God is chance, controls chance and invented and fathered chance. Chance, like the world, is subservient to God. God is over all.

In this midst, the world continues to have tragedies and misfortunes. As Job said with such faith, "Though he slays me, yet will I serve him." How can one say that? How can someone ever find happiness after such things as the world throws at us and God seemingly does not prevent it? It lies in faith, faith in the Word of God that we learned in Sunday School in those early years. Faith that we were exposed to when our grade school teachers would rise beside their desks and recite with us the Lord's Prayer.

The Bible stories are not sugar coated for that reason. God shows us what others did and how they coped with faith. David became "a man after God's own heart." Prior to that, he was a derelict, murderous, adulterous individual who sent a man into battle to die. Noah saved the world and proceeded to get drunk. The Apostle Paul, as Saul, like Moses, ~~were~~ was added to the list of murderers. They worshipped and God used them after the murders they committed.

God is not using some brand of human perfection to enter his kingdom. Everybody is welcome and nobody deserves it.

SWEET REPOSE, CASKET WIDE OPEN

The man said, "I want the casket wide open and I want to be splayed out in a new bright suit. My friends can marvel over the attire. That is what I want." This capsulized the burial of most in 1960's and 1970's. A big shebang, he called it. Later, on the death bed, a pronouncement was made, "it's all over but the shouting." Many adults said this during those dying times. This meant life was helpless, the grim reaper was soon arriving and there is nothing he can do about it.

Cremation was rarely mentioned as a type of burial. It was some northern thing or for the rich and the famous. "God is the only one that can burn you up "was the classic preacher response to the mere suggestion. This eliminated self-induced planning of cremation but not inadvertent burning trains, planes, or automobiles. Cremation simply speeds up the decomposition of the body and after getting over the initial shock of the urn instead of a casket, it became a modern approach as time passed.

Some used denim on the dead, in the agricultural community. High back overalls, as they were called, showed the life to be a hard working one. To save expense, many families gave the funeral home the clothes to use on the deceased. Others allowed the home to furnish the apparel which meant never with a pocket, never with shoes, socks, yes, no shoes. There are no pockets in a shroud, it was said. You cannot take it with you. No U haul trailers headed for the cemetery.

Funeralizing was done in segments, in compartments of action. There was the event, told and retold that took the life of the deceased, there was the selection process of caskets, chairs, flowers, clothes, ministers, pall bearers, even the diet of the week with high caloric meals of fried chicken and potatoes dispensed to the family at home and at the church fellowship hall. A southerner needs a proper burial, a proper funeral, and a proper eulogy. God forbid any mess-ups in any of the parts of the whole. The newspapers gave great lead in length of obituaries. The prominent and highly exalted could carry a whole column from top to bottom of the page if necessary. It would drone on and on, civic clubs, garden clubs, degrees, military service, church committees, political statements as the ink spilled along. I wondered if the small print was ever read and why the people always died in alphabetical order.

Then there was the service. It was said, "some were preached into heaven", other families were left to wonder just where the final resting place would be for their beloved. When a scoundrel died, the renegade brother threatened the preacher, "you call him a saint or I will cut you" The preacher, a loyal truthteller, could only think of one instance where he could say it. So, he did, he said, in the service, "compared to his brother there on the pew, this deceased man was a saint."

One minister droned on and on about the model citizen lying there in the casket, and all his good deeds, prompting his bereaved wife to come out of the bereavement state momentarily, lean over to her son and say," check the casket and see if that's your daddy in it, I believe they are talking about someone else."

The casket, pre burial, of course, had to be selected. In Chicago, caskets spanned a wall standing like soldiers in a line with the starting one a sarcophagus, a shallow box whose lid would crush the nose. The obvious inclination was that one could not breathe in that one. Sometimes there is a blurred line between reality and fiction in a mourning state. The widow could do nothing but burst into tears at the mental notion of a nose mashed flat by her choice of the final container. She wandered down toward the more substantial products led by the solemn funeral director, who in those years was called the mortician or undertaker.

Shopping for caskets after death is like shopping for groceries while hungry. You pay for overeating in one, overpay with grief in the other. Folks were encouraged to make the selection prior to their demise, but this rarely happened. It made folks to cognizant of their own mortality. Who wants to visit a funeral home and plan anything anyway? Just let it be part of the grieving process, let the family all meet over a dark oak table with a wire framed undertaker peering out of spectacles with a sheet of pricing and facts of body preservation and social security death benefits.

The family approached the preacher with a dilemma, "the undertaker has put daddy in a casket that we cannot pay for," they said. The preacher glanced at the casket sitting there in living room. It was shiny, that meant money, not a drab sullen fabric. It had just been rolled in by an undertaker who smoked outside. He resembled a long tall cigarette as viewed through the window. Large puffs of smoke through a yellowed pane, obscuring his features made him resemble a smoking pole. Smokers tend to look like cigarettes at some point, skinny, tall, and gaunt. Dogs and owners look alike from close contact. Married people tend to favor each other as well. It is one of life's many idiosyncrasies.

My dad, always looking out for the poor, replied to the family, "don't worry, I will handle it."

I said, "daddy, what will they bury him in?" Daddy said, "a cardboard box." I pondered that and imagined a large Kellogg's cereal box with a long lid, the eyes of the dead man peering into a cardboard top from within, pictures of frosted flakes on the backward cover. The visual was awful. I stuck close to hear the adults talking.

The family continued the discussion, "We cannot afford that coffin." My dad left the house and found the undertaker beneath a large oak in a cloud of smoke. "You need to take it back. ", he told him, "They cannot afford it." The undertaker was rattled and was perturbed, but held his peace. "Okay, okay" he said looking a little downtrodden, riches sprouting wings and flying away. The funeral man made a quick exit with the casket and the body.

Within two hours, the skinny undertaker in the tight black suit and long black hearse drove into the yard and parked in his same spot that he had left earlier. The deceased had been taken back to the starting point and returned two hours later in a dull fabric appearing casket. It was the one with a faded quilt covering. No shine. No reflection in the surface.

Indeed, it did feel like cardboard. I touched it and peered within. He still looked dead, none the worse for his swap and ride.

The corpse resumed his vigil under the mantle in the living room, the new black and white television sitting on top of the old one in the corner. Participants in chairs, with no order, around him, discussing LBJ's plan to remove poverty. There was a yard full of cars, a few on blocks and a washing machine on the porch. The plain yard was swept flat with an old broom. The death watch continued. In two nights, the mourning at the homeplace was over and the body was taken to the church for the service.

Six pallbearers carried the deceased into the church, always down the center aisle. One of the six said, "this handle is loose", as the casket was traversing the distance. I thought, "Yep, cheap casket, a paste board box." An hour later, the pallbearer said, upon leaving, "I told you it was loose, "as it pulled completely out of the side of the casket. He was left holding a handle in his hand as the director hustled to remove the confusion.

The line at the funeral home for the viewing could be long and winding. One exhausted elderly lady looked down into the casket and said, "This is not Beatrice." A quick investigation revealed that she was in the wrong line. Her deceased friend was several doors down in another room. Solemn attendants calmed the lady down and escorted her to the head of the correct grieving group. After seeing the new body, the lady said, "That's her." Relaxing with the sudden identification, she paid her respects and was hustled out, escorted to her car by the staff, shaking her head at the confusion.

FRIED CHICKEN, CORN BREAD, AND JESUS

In churches all over the South, revivals were standard faire yearly, sometimes twice yearly, fall and spring, sometimes fall only. Circulars and placards were printed, members were called upon and the message went out and was distributed on utility poles, store front windows and radio ads. It was a special time for rekindling of the souls. A week before the start of the event, a line formed in the foyer after the morning worship services. The women, never the men, were signing their family up to provide a meal for the incoming revivalist preacher. There were at least 10 meals with families. Each daily lunch and each supper or dinner as it was called, was around the table, at church family's homes. The evening meal preceded the evening revival service or gospel meeting as it was referred to. In this era, food was bought and prepared at home. There were no fast-food pickups, no gallons of tea purchased at a store. This was all homemade from scratch and much of the meal had been on the plant in the field the day or week before, like green beans or okra or squash. Many times, the families left the commodity on the plant in the field, until a day before the meal, in order to be completely fresh for the visiting preacher. One hospitable host lost the snap beans for the dinner because the Easter cold snap hit the field a day before the fellowship meal. The beans were frozen on the vine.

Conversations in these meals, at the homes, were the fore runner for the construction of the Fellowship Building on church properties in the 70's and 80's. The entire church could gather in a Fellowship Hall eliminating the need for the invited preacher to come home with them. The conversations in the church property were toned down and some of the character and depth of the meals was lost in this cultural shift. One could not shout frank talk of judgment or opinion fifty feet down the side of a long table in a room with 150 members. Some of the intimacy was lost.

The idea of a poor family having the preacher over was lost with the fellowship building. The humblest of homes had some of the best cooking for the preacher. In the meager circumstances, a white linen tablecloth graced the dining room setting. One small home with a few rooms, no heat other than a fireplace and no cooling other than a fan was the setting for one event. Christmas lights from a year ago were still on the eves, unlit. The patriarch of the family sitting at the end of the table in his chair, became unduly choked on a piece of chicken. This happens. It was a dramatic reversal of air and matter and the man had to jump up from the table. He ran to a nearby window and threw up from the screenless window out into the chicken yard. Chickens ran over to investigate their new found snack. The visiting preacher looked on with horror and nausea at the prospect of a man choking to death at the meal. The man survived and the chickens squalled and pecked underneath the dining room window. The patriarch returned to the table and continued without fanfare. The visiting preacher was aghast, gulped and covered up his trepidation.

Years of revivalist meals left many memories of the table fellowship, as church theologians call it today. The caloric content was in the thousands in any revival. Each family from the year before was known as a haven for some dish from a grandmother. It could be banana pudding, chicken and dumplings, sweet tea, fried chicken or the food of the gods, ambrosia. Ambrosia was always extinct after the grandmother or oldest member of the family died. The recipe died with her. It contained extra amounts of coconut, oranges slices, sauces of other fruit and other unknown or unrecorded items. It truly was an elitist food for royalty of long ago. Members gorged themselves and sent heavy waisted preachers into the pulpit two hours later with digestion in full attack. The preachers didn't care. Preachers were accustomed to eating and they never disappointed the host. You never heard of a gluten free preacher or some sensitivity to foods or allergy to the hundreds of calories that sat at that table. The word was "pass" as in pass the peas, pass the sweet potatoes, pass the whatever was swelling the air with an aroma of goodness.

There was love, fellowship, forgiveness and kindness exuding at the tables. Prayers were offered with blessings "for the hands that prepared it." And that is what Jesus wanted. It is not lost in study that Jesus, the son of God, spent his first night in a manger, a feeding trough. What a spectacular heavenly beginning. From humiliation of a feeding trough to an exultation within three years to the right hand of God, the Father in heaven. The ground is level at the fellowship table of sustenance, both spiritual and physical.

How did this come to be - this eating and drinking and socializing in a group family setting? It was devoid of racism and pessimism with the gathering of all classes of people around a basket of hot fried chicken or whatever was there. It's very complex, yet very simple. It was the way of Jesus. He brought it to earth from heaven when he came. It was an unorthodox manner of acceptance. The church leaders and Pharisees charged Jesus many times with associating and eating with sinners. They stood in their priestly attire, their religious symbols on display, as they gazed down their pious noses at the man from Nazareth. Jesus abhorred the policy of not inviting the lower and lessor of the world to these events. He stood firm behind those who were of lessor rank and circumstance. He freely intertwined with the ones who had bad reputations or social setting, the tax collectors, the prostitutes, the unclean as the church of that day called them. They were the outcasts, the ones that nobody wanted- the broken seashells on the beach, the dregs of the coffee pot, the street people, the unchurched who had left the church because of the attitude and treatment by the churched.

Jesus set the example of acceptance. He knew he could not initiate change without attaching himself to these people. But then he did more, much more. He gave sermons and presented a beautiful picture of a heavenly banquet when we would all be united in that last day, sitting around a spiritual table with Abraham, Moses and a host of witnesses who preceded us to heaven. He condemned a rich man who allowed a beggar to be hungry for years at his gate of the mansion, the man fared well while the beggar pleaded for food. He condemned a local church for forcing the poor to sit together in the assembly while the rich told of their escapades while avoiding any fellowship with the poor at the other end of the table.

Moses had commanded a meal of remembrance at a table, naming it Passover. This was a few hundred years before Jesus was born. It commemorated and brought to mind the escape from the Egyptian pharaoh through sea and over land. The Israelites marked the doorpost with blood of the lamb freeing them from the curse of death on their first born. The houses were passed over by the death angel. The Egyptians wailed and screamed, grieving over the plague of death that came upon them.

Hundreds of years later, the blood of a human lamb was shed, not at a doorpost on a home, but on a rugged cross as the Savior lay strapped, arms extended in an invitation to the world, dying for the sins of a world. God turned his back and darkened the sky at that instant, earth cracking open and dead saints walking around Jerusalem.

He took that same Table of Fellowship genre, the same one where he welcomed the world of misfits in a brief 36-month ministry, the same one where he was accused of drunkenness and debauchery by the Pharisees. He sat eating at a table with his disciples the night before he was crucified. In his most troubled time with the disciples shortly to be deserting him. He, he had a deep, visceral desire to take the Passover one more time before he met death. Miraculously, his disciples found a stranger who volunteered an upper room for the Passover meal. It was in this borrowed room, loaned by a stranger, where Jesus altered the Passover meal to allow for a new covenant, commanding the bread to signify his body and the wine to be his blood shed for forgiveness. It was this simple statement that led to more charges in years to come that the followers of Christ were cannibals.

From that day forward, after Jesus ascended to heaven, the ecclesia, the church body of believers, took the Lord's Supper often, when congregated and on the first day of the week. Even then, as Paul later warned, they had become oblivious of their behaviors and were commanded to be respectful of others and themselves. The event of Communion was so important that God gave Paul a heavenly recollection thirty years later with instructions for Christians to follow.

There's a wide encompassing spiritual heritage, extending through Old and New Testament scripture, covering rich and poor, from the Passover, ordained years ago. It was through the ministry of Jesus sitting at tables with the downtrodden and hated. It was with apostles the final night before he died. It was at all those caloric meals at the old revivals in the South. It was through church fellowship halls nationwide, through family meals at holidays, Christmas, Easter, Thanksgiving, and any other time two or three believers were eating together. It was the art of contemplating life, family, Jesus and what he desires for us to do.

This great earthly inheritance of opportunity, we today have received, will end with a spiritual banquet. The table will be the biggest ever built and the sight will be the lowly and the high mixed and mingling in equal rank as believers. It will be God's final leveling of humanity, where no presumption will be made on account of prestige, money or fame, but only in the simple belief that Jesus the Son of God came to earth to deliver to us, all of us, once and for all, a covenant that allowed us to break the bond of death and spend an eternity with our God and Savior. We will know each other as friends in the afterlife. There will be no tears and no cancer, no depression, no uneasiness, all the discomforts from minor to major will be terminated forever in that day. Death will have been finally eliminated along with all of life's problems. How can we neglect so great a salvation?

THE ILLUSTRATIONS OF ETERNITY

The choice was heaven or hell, decision- based Christianity. Man chose his destiny. This depended on the shift in the sermon related to Armenian or Calvinistic beliefs. `These were two schools of thought with multiple variations. The question was God's sovereignty and the responsibility of man in his decision for Christ. What position is man in if all has been predestined? Can he decide and go against the will of God? Yet, the Bible says, it is God's will that no one will perish. This led to many groups of thought and the discussion is not over yet. It has persisted for a few hundred years.

Somehow, we can say this with certainty, God is sovereign and knows everything past, present and future. On the other hand, man is called on to follow Christ. Salvation cannot happen without God and the Cross. These two schools of thought are certainly not an impossible situation for God and he can handle it. Jesus' last words were "Go into the world" We should honor his request.

In view of that, it fell on the preacher to describe the length of Hell or Heaven in human terms. The human mind is based on time, seconds, days, minutes, years. We live for the future. We look back at the past. There is no fathomable way for eternity to register completely in our thought process. Thus, illustrations were given using varying styles, types and emotions.

If the ant starts walking around the world, when he has worn down a path, eternity will have just begun. The thought of an ant making a path anywhere is pause for thought. Another was, if a bird flew from the earth to the moon and carried a grain of sand, when the earth was gone, eternity will have just begun.

There were thought provoking, scary and unsettling for children and adults, but the biggest scare we got came in 1965. A student who had been to a local country church revival recounted the illustration. The Baptist evangelist used the Mack Truck illustration. Forget the passive ant. This was a huge shiny massive truck that we all knew about and what it looked like. The story was told, as we gathered around her, a sixth-grade girl telling the illustration with wide eyed dramatic emphasis, that the Mack truck could top a hill and if you were hit head on, you would be launched into an eternity with the devil, if you were not saved. The preacher had said, "You could bust hell wide open." This was unsettling about getting busted by a Mack truck and then bust hell wide open. Weighing between the two, we considered this and became more afraid of the Mack truck than the eternity in hell.

She related that the preacher said what we would look like, after the truck hit. The car we were in would provide no protection and we would be folded up like Swiss cheese, whatever that meant. We would be bounced off the grill of the truck and pretty much burned up in the fiery crash projecting us into an eternity of hell, even though already incinerated.

We stopped caring about how long it would last, we were considering the fiery crash with bandaged up and missing extremities. We wanted to avoid hell for sure, but wanted to avoid a Mack truck catastrophe even more.

SCHISMS, SPLITS AND DIVISIONS

The armored truck maneuvered through traffic and stoplights to stop in front of the large church. Two uniformed guards briskly walked up the front steps meeting a church leader at the top with the morning contribution. This occurred immediately after the plate was passed. There was no time with the offering left piled up during the minister's sermon. The money bag was passed off to the armed guard and deposited through the back doors of the truck. The truck left. A few hours later, the same scene was repeated. Two groups were using the sanctuary on that Sunday morning. The judge's answer to the disagreement was to allow two worship services in the same building that day. A fair decision-secular style. It was undetermined if the use of the security truck was to prevent fellow Christians from taking the contribution or from non- Christian robbers from snatching it.

Seventy-five years ago, the member at church walked to the front and placed her contribution into the basket, under a white cloth with one hand, thus fulfilling "not to let the right hand know what the left hand is doing." (Matthew 6:3-4) A mild cultural change sent the basket carried through the sanctuary but not without some opposition to the status quo.

When Paul settled a Corinthian drunken disagreement with "you have homes to eat in", some took that to mean not one bit of digestion could occur in a sanctuary. It was unclear if chewing gum was allowed. It gets better. The Pharisees could not work on the Sabbath; thus, if a chicken worked by laying an egg on the Sabbath, the Pharisee would not eat it and would sell it to a Gentile. The Pharisees would also pay a Gentile to light the fire of wood which enabled the Pharisee to avoid working. The entire concept was a perversion of the intended law of God. Jesus came as the liberal to talk about the heart change, which is more difficult than checking boxes on a list.

The splitting of communion bread into small squares for consumption was of some concern. This was opposed by some due to the "breaking of bread" by Jesus at the initiation of the Lord's Supper, the night before he was crucified. The square was not broken, as it had already been broken off of a bigger piece.

Jesus' admonition to the disciples at that last supper, "Drink ye all of it.", has caused some to drink the amount completely of the communion, or be in violation by leaving some molecular elements in the bottom of the cup and losing salvation.

Calming churches down has now become an industry accompanied by seminars, studies, sermons, consultants and individual peace accords drawn up between two groups. One consultant said, profoundly, "It's a sin to divide unless it is a sin not to divide." That does have validity at some level. Another asked simply, "How will we all get along in heaven?" A good point.

Color caused many heated discussions and divisions in the 1960's and 70's. Skin color was the big one, kind of a moot point since Jesus died for all of us. Color of tile in the foyer, carpet color, fabric on the pew color, hard vs cushioned pews, circled or lined up, bulletin length, sermon length, hair length on the preacher, dress length on the preacher's wife, pants suits on Sunday morning, cremation or open casket, remodel or rebuild the old building, playground or not, bus ministry or not, size of cemetery next to a church, free lawn cutting by the members vs paid service provided by a brother in law of the preacher and on and on these discussions ensued. There are as many opinions available as there are issues. Hot business meetings have ensued. Numerous apologies have been said a week later.

One earnest member laid tile in the foyer as the men's business meeting, in another room, discussed what color tile should be bought. An energetic, angered member tried to cut a building in half with a chainsaw to prove his point of ownership. A few fists and slaps have been seen.

During a meeting at a divinity school where the discussion degenerated into controversy, one theologian took a pan of water and proceeded to wash the feet of every man in the meeting. This was a deeply spiritual experience. Afterall, we are supposed to be humble servants, not demanders of our own way. This made the group realize how petty some disagreements are.

It's not uncommon. It caused James to lament two thousand years ago, "What causes quarrels and fights among you?" (James 4:1) I am sure he was provided a list after his question. Paul and Barnabas parted ways initially over a heated discussion. Members were embroiled in Corinth. Poor people had to sit together down pew from the wealthy. Other problems in churches, including the Apostle Pauls' was favoritism by members of one preacher. Paul related that "he was glad he didn't baptize but two." (1 Cor. 1:14), thus creating less allegiance.

The disagreement and conflict place the world into the middle of the church, with the world's solutions enabling lawyers, speeches, sides and splits and filing of petitions.

A local church with the members is a loving, peaceful, generous group, until it is not. We expect God- full relationships to be easier on us than God-less relationships. Conflict can be expected however, since we are humans full of imperfections. The old adage is true, "if I found a perfect church, after my admittance, it would not be perfect."

The brick and mortar of the complex is fair game for a court battle. With multiple members contributing money for the construction of the building, the secular court can rule of a sale and a division of the sale proceeds or one group could buy the other one out. If there is no market for the building, the court may rule on joint use for a period of time. Judges are forced into church/state issues, with unsettled disagreements of members. Like all fights, it's a sad commentary on Christianity. Grace is needed, a continuation, not just one size fits all at a moment of salvation. It should be continuing throughout life.

Church descension is fodder for spiritual casualties of friendly fire. It can cause peaceful people to vacate the premises. A sixth-grade teacher remarked in 1965, to her class, that she was distraught over something in her small church. She had said silently in her church,

"God, I am here to worship and am not a part of the disagreement that came up this week." Children can be casualties in a broad way. Old enough to hear the home remarks about the troublemakers or being taken from Sunday School classes to different churches every year over disturbances place doubt into the child as to the "rock" that churches are supposed to be. It's sad.

It is an effort and struggle to avoid conflict because we all want our way. It makes one wonder though, as was said, "Can't we all just get along?", especially as believers. We need to realize that every issue is not a matter of salvation and is not worth fighting over. Putting Jesus ahead of us would solve most disputes.

CHURCHED AND DIVORCED

Forty years ago, at the end of the weekend visitation, the father stood behind the entry door to the hotel. A paper attached to the back of the door was frayed and mostly illegible. It told of some archaic room rents and traveler rules. It was posted well before any internet reservations and had the same authority as the mattress label that had printed, "Do not remove under penalty of law."

Two girls stood like skinny little soldiers and held the father's hand, knees straight, they prayed a prayer and the weekend visit ended. They wondered why he was there and who he was. The "Disney daddy", providing gifts and presents, throughout visits. How hollow does it sound to say? "See you in three months.", such Such is visitation with distance.

Hotel visitation became a problem because checkout was lunch and the visit needed to last longer. The social worker in the county was advised of the difficulty. After no solutions, she responded by finding a Presbyterian Church who volunteered to unlock their educational wing. The visitation occurred under the watchful eye of Moses and other colored pictures taped to the walls. There were no stipulations or rules pasted on a wall. We used craft supplies that were available. I have often thought that this church had no idea of the magnitude and help this gave to a father trying to exercise visitation a thousand miles from home. It solved a huge problem and gave me another half day with the children.

Churches in 60's 70's and 80's did not know what to do with divorced or divorcing members. Marriages were happy and fulfilling, till they weren't. Divorces were not the norm, but were increasing. When the courts jumped into the fracas with the advocate attorney, the marriage joy generally left. It was common for sides to be drawn and battle grounds to erupt. Theologians and churches proceeded cautiously, when the family could not be reassembled again. God was clear in Malachi, "God hates divorce." There were no good solutions forthcoming and churches avoided involvement.

Lost in the shuffle and in an effort for winners in the divorced to be chosen, the children sit idle, watching, waiting and suffering. No child was ever born and wished for a divorce or to be a pawn in a divorce action, a figurative slicing into two parts for parents. Many men just check out, leaving the marriage and the children behind.

In 1914, a father took one look into the cradle of his newborn son, walked out of the house into the cornfield, disappearing from view. Several family members watched. He left town and did not return. An older child saw him walking through the cornfield and spent the next few years peering from windows of cars, when cornfields were passed by, looking for "daddy" among the corn stalks. Daddy never came home.

On the battlefield of divorce, the figure standing in the mist, obscured by the fog of accusations and hurling of hate, by the parties involved, is the child. Eventually, the mist clears, the dust settles and a lawyer or judge pronounces a victor. There is left, a wasteland, with smoking piles of refuse and burned-out buildings, a war zone. Some of this is unavoidable, some is not.

In the front of the scene, children are standing, waiting for their uncertain future. The children will grow up, regardless of the environment, good or bad. They will still grow, but will mature with values and goals of what they have been taught and what they have seen. At some point, they will make their decisions about life, and they will pray that they are never divorced, once married.

In those years, divorced members were sometimes denied communion, not allowed in any positions of leadership, no church office or in a volunteer capacity. No complaints were lodged by church members if the divorced were placed in prison ministry outreach. Whether preachers like it or not, whether lawyers are pleased or not, there is redemption in this mix somewhere, more than man will allow. The Bible is full of second chances given by God over the objections of men in scripture. Saul the murderer, became Paul the Apostle, over the objections of many. God's answer to sin and mistakes has always been redemption, through what Jesus did on the cross.

CHURCHED AND COLLEGE

It was a shower room for the freshmen, I was alone under a running shower. A boy entered and turned on his shower, the steam emerged and filled the room. He turned and said, "Could you test this water so that I won't get burned, I have no pain fibers in my body." Without a second thought, I extended my hand in the water and said, "Its fine." The helpful southerner that I was. Or maybe just naïve. The boy screamed with delight and had a paroxysm of laughter, then jumped under his shower. Welcome to college.

It was 1971. I was a preacher's kid and a principal's kid and tried to live up to the name. There were many boundaries and hedges, which I jumped. I had a propensity for occasional, unwise behavior. Bearing this in consideration, the wisdom of my parents intervened, they said that they would pay for a close state school in Georgia or a Christian college, Harding College, in Searcy, Arkansas. Both parents had attended there. I chose Harding to get away. I gladly left Georgia and my parents, bound for Arkansas. I spent the rest of my life trying to get back into the dirt, blowing gnats, and living among pine trees in South Georgia. Thank God that I chose Harding. It crystalized my foundation and prevented a host of eternal disasters in future years.

After about 24 hours in the dormitory room, the responsibility comes home or lack thereof. Realization that the student has no one determining if the alarm clock goes off or when the night lights go out can excite a youth to near hysteria. It actually registers about thirty minutes after your parents leave the campus. Some react with such joy that they last less than a semester. They go home, move in and try to grow some values for a year. Many are back to a college in a year, some are not. The idea of suddenly being away from parental control is overwhelming for some, and they never recover, jumping head first into all kinds of misdeeds that originate from outside parental control.

The Vietnam War was raging. We were all 18 and had registered for the Selective Service. Deferments were given for educational attendance. The television in the dorm lounge had nonstop black and white coverage of the war. I suspected that may have driven some to college while some enlisted to serve their country. Long hair was common and stood for a rebellion and the revolt against the status quo. Many of us tucked it behind our ears and used various preparations at Harding College to obscure the length. It worked to a degree. There was a hair and dress code. We studied, we took large schedules of courses, attended chapel daily and church on Sunday.

The church sanctuary had about a thousand in attendance for a service. Never had males seen so much beauty under one roof. It was enough to lead some to immediate conversions. The first letter home from Harding to parents usually made mention of the large number of beautiful Christian females.

In the Sunday service, it was noticed that about 20-30 students would migrate out after the Communion, conveniently before the sermon. Various side doors and exits would accommodate them silently and quickly. I followed this for a few weeks, then asked. "Oh", a thoughtful student said, "They are taking communion and avoiding the sermon." I responded, "Can we do that?" I was incredulous and realized again how naïve I was. I had to ponder the meaning of that for a while.

Somehow, rebellion seeks its own group and one migrates to another. Some of us wanted to look like the drug culture, but we were not. There were no drugs and we didn't want any. However, we wanted hair long flowing and flaxen as sung in the song, Aquarius. We wanted rock music, loud, bold and rebellious. We wanted bell bottoms jeans and denim attire. We wanted old military coats from thrift stories. We were a rugged, appearing, motley crew.

On Saturday morning, we would hitch rides on the interstate to Little Rock, being transported by a host of amiable drivers. Thumbs raised; drivers would pull up easily. It was a different time. We would arrive at Little Rock, buy a 4-dollar ticket and line up at Barton Colosseum. Six hours later, we were seated on the floor, ten feet from any one of a host of acts that toured those years, James Taylor, Ike and Tina Turner, Black Oak Arkansas, Grand Funk Railroad, Canned Heat, Isaac Hayes, Edgar Winter's White Trash, Johnny Winter and others.

We watched a rowdy fan attempt a dance with Tina Turner during Proud Mary. She kept singing and the saxophone players kept playing as they kicked him from the stage. He fell harmlessly off into the darkness. In most concerts, the smell of marijuana wafted through the air. We did not partake. We were already so wild; we did not want to be pushed into total insanity

We were content with our cultural uniforms, the denim, torn tee shirts and our rebellious attitudes. We were required at Harding College to be clean cut, a few of us had to have a haircut at registration. I had two the same day. In one encounter with the Dean, I admonished him that I simply wanted my hair like the pictures hanging in the hallway of Barton W Stone, Thomas Jefferson and Jesus. That conversation did not go well. Facing a return to Georgia, I was sheared a second time. Thirty-five years later, I crossed paths with the dean at a church in New York City and gave a reserved apology for my attitude years earlier. He feigned ignorance, but I suspected he might remember. Interestingly, now the hair code is shoulder length, 51 years later. Cultures change, generations change, times change, hair still grows.

Studying one night for biology, I was interrupted by a friend who asked me to cut a thread on the seat in front of me, during chapel service the next day. I kept studying, barely acknowledged him, and said, "whatever." The next day, I was surprised to find a black clothing thread, attached to the back of the theater seat in front of me, almost invisible, traveling upward to the ceiling. The chapel was not well lit and this was inconspicuous. I leaned forward during the service and popped the string, insignificantly.

To my sheer horror, in front of a thousand-person audience, the string disappeared into the ceiling. Ribbons of toilet paper, in a row, unfolded down across the entire front of the auditorium, extending their length and drifting slightly in the atmosphere, slightly above the heads of the audience. It was horrendous and I was mortified.

As the strips of toilet paper fell, a known fire and brimstone preacher, a PhD in Bible, shouted from the front row, "They're in the front balcony, I will get them!". He then sprinted up some circular stairs on the stage, taking huge leaps and arriving to an empty balcony. He walked down slower, dejected. "No one is there." He remarked and sat down. The interruption was brief, and normalcy resumed, but the strips of toilet paper maintained a vigil until we walked out. I was surprised that the doors were not locked, chapel suspended, and the guilt ridden ordered to hit the front row, or sit there all day.

I was never advised as to how a prank with that much engineering was attained. I resolved to never pull an unknown string. I decided, this was a scene, designed by some intelligent, engineering mind, a feat of physics and gravity. I had strong suspicions. No confessions were made. No repentance surfaced. I disappeared into the masses at Chapel that day and acted as shocked as everyone else over the spectacle, obviously caused by renegades. "How reckless," I opined. No comments were ever heard and the incident disappeared from history.

It was a hot summer, college break in South Georgia in 1973. The travel trailer had meager axels and the contents were sparse. The star sat on a bed with a headful of hair extending a foot in all directions. He was flying through guitar sets with fingers that violated the laws of physics, practicing for the show in an hour. This was silently done with no amplifier. Other band members chilled and sat on another sofa. The headline act was Ted Nugent and the Amboy Dukes, from Detroit. Due to the promoter, I wound up shoved into the trailer to watch prep for the opening act. I was in awe. Ted Nugent was already an icon in the music industry and over the last forty years became famous for conservative values, hunting and avoidance of drugs. He continues to tour and please thousands of fans. He is an American IIero.

HONORABLE CONGRESSMAN
WILBUR MILLS

I stood dapper in a suit in the office of Congressman Mills from Arkansas. The suit was complete with tie and shined shoes. The outfit looked like a Sunday morning. He signed numerous papers on a huge desk, as I told him what I wanted. He went from one to the other without looking up, yet he answered my questions with gracious patience. I explained that I was in a freshman political science class at Harding College and wanted to occasionally come to his office and be exposed to his work. I related that I had an interest in law. While signing, he waxed on about public work, politics, the job, the prior job as a judge and current status of head of the Ways and Means Committee in Washington DC, in Congress.

I didn't tell him that I had seen his picture in U S News and World Report. Already, I knew everything about him. I knew he spoke with President Nixon frequently and was a powerful man in the structure of Washington, D. C. "Powerful" was always the adjective used by the press in any article about Wilbur Mills. He had been in Congress for thirty years having run for office as a judge in Arkansas. He was elected to the Arkansas 2nd congressional district in 1939. He was from miniscule Kensett, Arkansas outside Searcy and supported all pork barrel policies for his district. His stature was huge and he was loved by Arkansans.

I made this trip several mornings in the semester. He spoke with me every session and the secretary were patient with my calls. I had been told that 80 percent of life was just showing up and I have found that to be true. Don't make an appointment, just go there. State your case. Hope for the best. Accept the worst. Show personal involvement. Forget phone calls or cards.

I told Congressman Mills that I would like to do a story on him for the newspaper of Harding, The Harding Bison. The congressman had always supported the colleges in Arkansas. As was usual for me, I showed up at his home in Kensett, unannounced. After I knocked, the door was opened by his wife, a petit woman with a gentle smile. She said, "Oh, he will have to do it later, we have Earl Warren over for supper now." I could see Mr. Warren through the door opening. I was transfixed for a moment, Earl Warren, The Earl Warren, The Chairman of the Warren Commission, the famous Supreme Court Justice. Wow, what a story to remember. I left, unable to meet him. Attendance only goes so far. I did gaze, upon leaving, on a light-colored Mercedes, Washington DC, the single number 1 on the tag. Wow was all I could muster. I did the interview with Congressman Mills later and it was published in The Bison in 1973. When I told my college friend about it, he related that he had walked by Earl Warren's house in Hayward, California for years on his way to 8th – 10th grade.

A few months later, I crossed paths with the Congressman at the hospital where I worked part time as an orderly. A member of his family had been assigned to me as a patient. I was unaware of the relationship until he came to the room late one night. I assisted him to the elevator to leave, we went down together. We talked, he looked up and said, "Would you like to go to law school in Arkansas." "I can help you out." I was floored and somewhat disappointed, as I had assumed that I would never get in.

I told him that I had decided to go into podiatry. He said, "~~that's~~ That's good." He left and I never saw him again. I enjoyed the relationship and he was a statesman for sure, in the company of presidents and princes. He was a mover and a shaker in Washington D. C.

He had put together many bills as head of Ways and Means - Medicare, Social Security, Medicaid, and numerous tax bills. He had power, prestige, seniority and the electorate loved him, for thirty years.

A year later, the Congressman suffered a political setback with an encounter with Fannie Foxe, a stripper at The Silver Slipper, in DC. Alcohol was certainly involved, as were police and the entire press of Washington D. C. The dive by Fannie, into the Tidal Basin, in the early hours of October 9, 1974, sealed his fate. "A lovers quarrel", as was later described. An appearance on a stage with her a few weeks later sealed his political destiny. The Congressman ultimately did not run again, entered rehab and lived out his days. Fannie became the "Tidal Basin Bombshell" and had a career.

On a bizarre note, I went on to Chicago for my

education and was working years later in the Drake Hotel. I was sent to carry the baggage of a party of two beautiful women. I listened to the conversation as one said to the other, "What did you think of your picture being on the front page of the Chicago newspapers?"

At that point, I was tipped, secured the two a cab, and they rode away. I quickly located the Sun Times and found on a prominent page, Fannie Foxe, who had been spotted in Chicago. Well, I thought, if I had known that, I could have told her that I was friends with Wilbur and maybe I could have gotten a better tip. What paths we do cross in life. There are no coincidences.

EXPOSURE TO SUFFERING

The father and mother stood outside of a large plate glass window at the hospital nursery. Silent. Observing. No conversation. The baby had no visible signs of any problem. As they watched, a nurse gave him a bottle. He seemed content. He was wrapped tightly in the standard, flannel, hospital blanket in 1973. The couple held each other tightly, obviously moved, and upset. Still silent. Other infants, in view of the window, slept quietly.

I was a newly hired hospital orderly and was standing behind them. The Arkansas hospital had hired me with no training, other than the last few days of orientation. This was standard fare, on the job instruction. I had decided that motivation and a beating heart were the two main requirements, which seemed to apply to most jobs. Motivation was the most important. Just show up. I used the advice of a friend who told me what to say. He instructed, "go to the interview, let it proceed, and let your final words be, someone in your hospital is not doing their job, and I want their job."

He said his father had instructed that the phrase was a "guarantee to make them think of someone who was lazy and unneeded in the company." It sounded plausible. It did let me leave the interview having dropped a weight on them that they might not have heard before. Sure enough, I got the job two days later in a phone call. It was a part time job. I was in college.

We know from elementary school science books, the name Louis Pasteur and his little creatures that he called germs. We learned of Alexander Fleming and his penicillin discovery. But there is another part to hospitalization and medical treatment that I would learn. To stagger in sick and leap out well or a variation thereof, a set of circumstances has to happen. There must not be variance from the standard of care. The correct name must receive the correct medication. Rest is needed but too much is bad. Bedpans should be at a reasonable temperature. The staff must stay at least partially behaved. These parts are the human part, when we place ourselves in the care of the mercenary service that is hired to care for the sick.

Now, I stood in my costume. I had a name badge, white pants, white shirt, pure looking, with absolutely no idea at what I was supposed to do or how to act. In the bright white, I looked cleaner than I really was. I smiled, hiding my ignorance. It always worked. Already, I had found that I would be faced with multiple emotional events of which I had no idea how to respond. I looked the part, and was convinced if I kept the serious, strained look, with some smiles, I would be considered a trained health professional and drift in and out of patient rooms with my meager assignments. Hopefully, I would receive no questions that would require knowledge, discussion or a remote opinion.

Shortly, a nurse appeared at the end of the corridor and motioned for me to follow. She led me through a maze and into the back of the nursery. She had something to "show me." The window blind to the nursery was now tightly closed. We were alone, the contented baby, the nurse and myself. She was unwrapping the baby for a diaper change. She laid him briefly on his stomach, pulling the diaper down and revealing a reddish oval opening into the body, lower spine. It was naked, an area of red tissue, about an inch long, confined to the opening. There was no swelling or infection to indicate that this was anything but normal. I stared and gulped.

She said, "this is spina bifida, and that is why the parents were upset." She explained the deformity, as being possible sensory loss below the waist and a lifetime of disability, of some degree. "There is no cure." she explained. It was the first of many times that I would hear that explanation in healthcare.

I left shaken, as any 20-year-old would be. I had some conviction, but no real understanding. Deeply, in my own adolescent, immature way, I wondered how the parents would handle this. I also wondered how we got to this point. What happened? I filed the uncertainty away and continued my work that night.

Forty-nine years later, on a Tuesday night, August 19, 2022, I stood with my daughter and her husband over their child, my grandson, Wells. He was 13 months old, having just been diagnosed with Joubert's Syndrome, a rare genetic disorder, in which part of the cerebellum is missing. My grandson now faced his own lifetime of procedures and uncertainty.

As the diagnosis was rendered by the MRI, the "molar sign" indicating cerebellum malformation, in a flash, I was transported back to that night when I saw the baby with spina bifida. I gulped again, this time looking now down at my grandchild, not their child. I was strangled by the memory that rose up. Fate had bound and linked me with their pain, uncertainty, and doubt. Suddenly, I did feel their pain. They did not know me; I did not know them. I wondered how they managed, how the baby did, and a host of other questions that would never be answered in this life. Now, I was in their universe, standing with them, suffering as they had suffered, supporting each other, unknowingly.

Twenty patients were assigned nightly to myself and an RN. We were charged with their care. The work shift was 3-11 PM. This was an excellent period, with all the main bosses and managers at home in bed, exhausted from their previous eight hours, unconcerned about a white suited boy wandering the halls in ignorance and on their payroll. I had been advised of this benefit by a senior old nurse who advised me to take that shift. She became my mentor and confidant. Her advice was dead on, as I found out.

The care was given with the patient, living or dead. My work was mostly hands on type work, movement of bedpans, urinals, lab equipment, covering of naked patients, with blankets, some deceased, inserting enemas, urinary catheters, locating IV bags of strange looking fluid. It was a much more intimate involvement than I had imagined. I was curiously apprehensive and expectant at the same time. Through high school, I had experience in farm work, cows, feeding horses, washing dishes in restaurants, and selling and stocking clothes in a clothing store. I had no knowledge of anything related to anybody's health.

The rumor of my new job and knowledge flew like lightning through the dormitory and I became the "go to" person for any question about a body in the student body. These encounters were late at night, knocking quietly on the door, asking me about swellings and drainages and colors. It was an interest in my new found knowledge, or so it appeared. I feigned ignorance, mostly, an easy thing to do, but could invent some disease or cure, if I was really demanded to impress. I would compare their infirmity to something serious and deadly. I would then tell them to seek care. Quick.

At the hospital, with my clip board in hand, I had to ask pertinent questions. "Have your bowels moved today?" I avoided the eyes when I asked that question. Briefly, I managed a direct stare. I never understood that question, to move sounded like a state away, not a part of an intestinal makeup. I wanted to lie on the floor and enjoy a seizure of laughter when I asked the question. "Have your bowels moved today? ""Well, yes, they went to Minnesota, but made it back on the bus early this morning."

I took 20 blood pressures a night from 20 anxious patients, all eager to hear the verdict. In those days, it was privileged information and not shared with the patient, since it could be upsetting. Patients were not allowed to know everything about their body. Part of early medicine was a mysterious component where patients were not told of their own diagnoses. Doctors routinely acquiesced to families who did not want mama to know that she had a tumor or cancer or other maladies. Some doctors rebelled at this and advised the families that it was the doctor's obligation to tell the patient what problem the patient had.

At the hospital, I was intrigued to learn that the patient's life story was composed and typed neatly in a binder, called a chart, and was available under the term "history." I spent hours reading all the charts, looking at lab work, reading social histories and medical diagnoses with symptoms. I came to realize that a person could be diagnosed by studying the data. I was amazed at what a minor complaint could reveal. The stories themselves were a combination of data and sad intervals with clues of symptoms sometimes over a ten-year period of time.

A headache could be a brain tumor, burning hands and feet - diabetes or B12 deficiency, weight gain - overeating or pregnancy, calf pain- a blood clot. Indigestion- minor stomach ulcers or myocardial infarction. I continued reading late into the night in the hospital. It was better than my literature class.

One of the doctors said that 80 percent of diseases are self-limiting. He explained that meant they would improve over time with little treatment. The 20 percent is what would put you under. I found that interesting.

One thing became apparent really quick. A person can look like a picture of health and be a dead man walking. From nowhere, death comes to those who look like life. To those that don't know, it arrives. The grim reaper makes the rounds on the healthy. Many folks do get sick and die. At least they had a warning, subtle or not. Others are living life to the fullest, and they drop dead. I wondered if they were the fortunate ones, the ones that did not know it was coming. As I read the patient histories, I realized that there was a lot about the world that I did not know.

I was shocked at what could befall a human being. All manner of accidents, bacteria, viruses, infections and the scariest of all, walking pneumonia, whatever that was, which killed you quick as you trudged along, feeling not dapper, but certainly not deadly. Then, you breathed your last breath. It was in that second week of work, that I was sent to the Emergency Department when I clocked in.

One patient and his healthy, visiting wife, had succumbed to pneumonia within hours of each other. I had spent afternoons with them in their tiny hospital room, breathing their breaths and laughing at their humor. Then, within a day or two, they died. Post mortem revealed galloping pneumonia. I galloped to the ER and received a shot of gamma globulin, painful, and in each naked hip. It felt like being shot with syrup as it expanded in the closed space of my body. In 1973, in some scientific study far away, it was learned that gamma globulin injections had allowed some exposed to pneumonia to live. I took the shots and did not die. It was my first encounter with the grim reaper at the periphery of my young life and as with all of us, there would be more.

HOSPITAL PROTOCOL

Addressing a newly hired worker for the hospital, the nurse said, "you are assigned to him." She pointed at me, as if I was the fountain of all thing's hospital related. I feigned reluctant interest and shook the boy's hand. The nurse left. We then had a good laugh, as our scheme had worked. He applied for the same type of job that I had, and was a fellow student at Harding College. The plan was that we would work together with the management not realizing that we were friends. We figured it would be better that way. He was now my partner in crime or whatever appeared on the horizon. I felt that two knowing nothing was better than one lone ranger.

I was quickly assigned an enema with instructions to train my newly hired friend. I learned, only a week earlier, that an enema was the introduction of a massive amount of fluid into the body for purposes of flushing out the intestinal tract for investigation of a problem. Outside of the patient's room, the procedure was called a 3 H procedure. Hot, high, and a heck of a lot. All Hs were understated. In fact, it was 1500 cc's with 500cc given while lying on the left side, 500cc given while lying on right side, and 500cc while lying supine position. The patient would then either burp salt or soap, midway thought it, depending on what solution was in the bucket. Either packets of soap or packets of salt were used.

I imagine that today, 50 years later, that amount is medically irresponsible or illegal in most states and a few foreign countries. Back then it was a true colon cleansing. Since that time, it has been propagated that an amount that large, entered into the body, could be harmful. The newly hired friend related that he knew "how to do it." We were on our way. Our first assignment together.

I showed him how to requisition and gather the bucket, tubes, soap, and paraphernalia to perform the procedure on the patient, ensuring the patient would be charged his fair share of the health care system. We entered the room as if we were trained professionals. The victim, or rather patient, as he would prefer to be called, was a small, thin man without an ounce of fat on his frame. It seemed that he would be the least likely person to need anything removed by irrigation or force. He appeared to need all the parts and weights of his body. He was also rather old, and not looking too kindly on a tube being entered into his residence. He took the announcement grimly, as we informed that we were his healthcare team ready to perform an enema. I thought of a prior patient, when hearing a knock on the door, remarked, "Is this friend or enema?"

The patient, with reluctance, laid on the bed in the appropriate positions, eyes wide, and was fast receiving his last of the 1500 cc's when he grimaced and said, "I got to go." He did not ask permission. He mobilized and swung his feet off the bed while sprinting to the bathroom. In a methodical and knowing manner, my friend removed the tube from the bucket and dropped the tube to the floor. As the patient gained speed, with obvious spasms and abdominal cramping, the tube was following behind him, like a long tail in a Charles Darwin like state. Quietly, I leaned over to my trainee and said, "you must remove the tube from the man's bottom and not the bucket." "He cannot go to the bathroom with the tube still in him."

He looked at me with an incredulous expression and said, "Oh." He received the statement with horror and his confidence was eviscerated. His slow, methodical persona was dashed. My friend leaped to the floor, as if going for a ground ball in a World Series. Chairs, blankets, and bedding were thrown asunder, as we both scrambled. He grasped the long tube, stood partially up, and pulled it out of the man, jerking, in a form that resembled bringing a large flounder into an unsteady boat on a seafaring expedition.

As the flounder landed on the deck, Isaac Newton's law went full force, and like the apple, hastily dropped. Then, physics took over. A jet propulsion of water that would power the Hoover Dam was expelled containing 1500 ccs of liquid and other body parts and seams. My friend grabbed a huge towel and covered, as best he could, the man's small posterior. It was to no avail. By the time the patient made it to the commode, most of the experiment lay on the floor. We cleaned with multiple towels and mopped quickly to avoid some senior employee firing us on the spot.

A simple enema had transformed the room into a battle zone resembling a small country. We quickly sanitized the room and pronounced the patient all done, thanking him profusely for being so nice and understanding. We wished him luck in his procedure scheduled in 24 hours. We hoped and prayed that he would think what happened was a standard enema with no surprises. Hopefully, he had never had one performed and didn't know any better. We waited for reprimands or firings, but a week went by with no negative feedback. Safe. We relaxed. Our ignorance was still unknown to the masses. We breathed a sigh of relief and went on to our next adventure.

A CASE OF MISTAKEN IDENTITY

One evening, my vast experience in the hospital world led me to be assigned "post-partum." I asked what that was, and she replied, "care of the mother post-birth." I grimaced and asked, "What In the world could I possibly do to assist a suffering woman with a bad stomach ache?" She quipped, "you will do nothing when you answer the call, because they will see you are a male, you will present a bedpan and they will certainly place it under themselves, and dismiss you immediately." This sounded easy and I relished the idea of getting paid to read charts at the nursing station.

I sat and immediately began reading about a host of symptoms that pointed to leukemia, though unconfirmed. My session was interrupted with a loud buzzer down the hall. I found the woman, calm, cool and collected, with a strange statement, "The nursery brought me my baby, but it is not my baby." As she said this, she was holding a neatly wrapped infant in her arms, protectively, and the baby had no complaints.

She was one of these people that rarely gets upset, she sounded as if she could be asking for a television adjustment. However, I destroyed her patience and manner when I asked the question that only a dumb 20 year could ask in such a situation. "How do you know?" She then screamed," "I know my baby."

I ran sensing some urgency and hastily returned to the nursing station. I was a little breathless, sensing come some coming excitement and said, to a group of women, charting papers and filing their nails, "The lady in 214 says the baby she has been given, from the nursery is not, hers." You would think I had said the building was on fire. The group jumped up, and fell all over themselves running to the room, hitting the door full force, all entered and crowded around the bed.

A quick investigation revealed that she was correct. Her baby, born that's morning, was sent hours earlier with a family home to their country abode in Arkansas. The baby she held, was several days old and the arm band had been removed in error that morning.

The staff ran back to the station and I watched the melee. A nurse that I always characterized as "prude following the rules" took charge of the error. She called the administrator and told him of the dastardly deed. He yelled into the phone, "Don't anybody move, until I arrive. "

My old nurse confidant grabbed me and we disappeared into a linen room with a phone. She closed the door. She said to me, "I know those country people that we gave the baby to." "I will get that baby back before that administrator comes in here and fires us all." She called and gently advised the parents that they had been given the wrong baby hours earlier. They were humble people and were mortified. She said, "Hurry back." So, we then walked out and returned to the desk as the group we had left was reaching full, nuclear, melt down. Tears, excuses, shock, horror. "How could this happen?", they retorted.

My friend and I sat quietly staring at the elevator doors in front of the station. There was a noise, the doors opened, there stood a woman holding an infant accompanied by a denim dressed man, both looking sheepish and unknowing what to do.

My friend and I had secretly told the mother of the missing child to walk with the baby down to the elevator. The couple stepped off. Within seconds, the lady stepped forward extending their baby. The swap went off without problem. Within another 30 seconds, the couple disappeared with their real child, leaving the mother to kiss her baby now in her arms.

As the couple got off the elevator with the baby, Miss Prude, following the rules, was astounded and upset. "Who called the family?" She spoke. A discussion could not follow because all eyes were on the swap. No one said a word.

Literally one minute later, as the couple left, the doors opened and a harried, disheveled administrator leaped off, "Where's the baby, where are they?" he yelled. The nurse said, "the swap is done". He screamed, "I told you to wait till I got here." His shoulders sagged; he resembled a defeated collapse. All heads studied the floor and he disappeared with a couple of nurses down the hall lecturing angrily.

After work that night, when I returned to my dorm room, my roommate was asleep. I looked into the dimly lit mirror, studied my face, and said, "Am I who I think I am?" I went to bed, the question unanswered to this day.

DEATH, BUGS AND A FAKE DOCTOR

The patient died. I had been assigned a gentle, overweight, male, the day before. He was not demanding, not rude. He seemed pleasant and healthy and had died overnight. Since my introduction, as an orderly to his care, he developed some kind of heart ailment that flared up and killed him in 24 hours. I entered the room. The window was open. A gentle breeze was blowing over the body and rustling the sheets. He seemed at peace and asleep. Eyes were closed. No family was in the room. They had already left., tThe previous night, I had stood by the bed and chatted with the nice man. At that time, he inhaled and exhaled, his rotund stomach rising and falling. He had now inhaled and exhaled one last time. The stomach lay still. I thought, as I contemplated this, that it would be true for all of us. We would inhale and exhale one last time. In my youth, the thought vanished.

The funeral home was enroute. The room was clean, no odors, no fluids, no sign of a struggle with life. No visible signs that he had left his earthly home. A peaceful death. He passed away when the heart quit beating. There seemed to be some consolation in that for me. His gentle demeanor had carried him on out. I remembered him as a kind man.

I walked by another room and heard a man telling the nurse, "I'm not the Smith that is on insulin." "He is in the other bed, next to me." I thought, why in the world, would you put two people with the same last name in one room? He spent his entire stay refusing treatments, needles and dietary restrictions.

My friend's second enema that he installed had a small aberration. For conversation, as the country boy laid on the bed, he asked why enemas were given. At this point, 1500 ccs were being installed My friend remarked that it would "get the bugs out." I grimaced, wondering how the patient would take that cool explanation.

I guess that could be a good a reason as any. It had an undesired effect on the country boy. "What," he hollered, "Do I have bugs in me?" With a frantic, shaken, high pitched voice, he yelled and proceeded to grasp the tube and pull it straight out of his body. My friend assured him there were no real bugs in his intestines. It was time to go anyway, but this threw a little unexpected drama into the procedure. I left my friend cleaning up another trail to the bathroom.

A severe complication of multiple sclerosis can cause loss of sensation in the body. A pretty female in her 60's was bed confined from the ravages of MS at an early age. The nerves didn't work to allow mobility and sores developed from the neuropathy. Wearing gloves, I applied ointment to her ulcers and I held back grimacing from her condition. Life has never been fair. Eternity for the believer will be.

A 30-year-old had a stroke at age 22 and was bed

confined. The stroke caused paralysis on one side. The extremity had atrophied and shrunk the entire limb. The limb was in considerable pain from neuritis due to the stroke. H could barely be touched. He said, "Can you do something for me?" He then used the good hand to lift himself sideways, as I wedged a foam piece under his entire raised side, allowing him to change position. The little things that we don't think about are sometimes eliminated with failure of our health. A simple turning of the body. Imagine sleeping all night in one position. This pathology is also present in amyotrophic lateral sclerosis, ALS. The mind is alive and the body is failing. I couldn't sleep that night.

A cardiologist would refuse nursing assistance and do all his exams alone with the patient. The cardiologist would turn down any nursing staff help. This was not uncommon but a little unusual. As he entered a room and disappeared, my mentor, the old nurse who confided in me, said. "He is not a doctor, that is a son of a family in another part of the state." I was only 20, but I was flabbergasted. "A fake doctor!" I said, as she pointed her bony finger at the man. She took me aside and said not to tell anybody because we could lose our jobs. I didn't want that, so I, with the maturity of a walnut, did just that. I went about my business and didn't tell a soul that a marauder with no credentials was herding up consults and listening to hearts.

A week later, I was working in the emergency room, I loved it and rarely was assigned there. There sitting on the exam table was the assumed fake doctor as a patient, with a stomach ache. He looked at me and pointed at a pen holder in my pocket inscribed with Tylenol on it and said, "Tylenol, that's a funny name for a person."

I laughed and decided he was the faker and had bad jokes. I didn't breathe a word. A few minutes later, he was examined by the ER doctor for his apparent appendicitis. The real doctor was suspicious of the bad joke doctor and asked about his relationship to a hospital in Little Rock. The faker said, "Oh yes, I am there all the time." The doctor returned after making a phone call, and said, "I called the hospital, and they have never heard of you." The man grabbed his possessions up and sprinted out of the ER, suddenly improved with his acute stomach. He screeched away in his car. He had maintained the fake consulting doctor routine from the big city for several months. He had somehow, befriended and convinced other doctors that he was a renowned cardiologist. What a joke.

The ruse lasted, until it didn't. He was caught and prosecuted. I never told anyone that the old nurse had told me weeks earlier. Actually, I had not believed her until I saw him running frantically out of the ER, clothes flapping and jumping into his car.

I was working in unknown and unchartered territory, in a landscape that I had never seen, with the dead and the sick. I filed the fake doctor story away, but said little. Each new work period held new information. I was way down the food chain making 1.75 an hour. There was no way that I was going to volunteer information that a doctor was a fake. What did I know? I needed my job.

BATH FAILURE

Perhaps the biggest blunder was a bedside bath failure. Generally, you set it up and the patients would sponge bathe themselves. This suited the assigned orderly appropriately. Less work. In this case, the man wanted himself bathed by a trained professional. He did not know that they were in short supply. The day before, a perky, blonde nurse had bathed him, much to his delight. I surmised, when he saw my face, that he wanted a blond instead of a dark-haired man. She was busy, I don't think she wanted him back. To speed this process along, I started scrubbing and moving water onto his body in an overzealous manner that used way too much liquid soap. When realization hit, I knew I was in trouble, past the point of no return. I had a 300-pound male covered in enough lather to wash 10 people, and that was on the part of his body that was exposed. His back had not yet been touched. Where is a pressure washer when you need one? The man was big, a lot of square skin footage and area.

I commenced to start at the toes with wet towels removing the residue and soap. It rapidly escalated, such that I had not only too much soap, but too much water. A double difficulty. It was a bedside disaster. I circled the wagons and called for reinforcements. We had to remove the patient from the bed, attempt a chair bathing and change the soaking wet sheets to return him to the bed. I hastily left. He was mad as the proverbial wet hen, a heart patient, and his face was red as a beet. Not a good sign. I thought he might die, at my hands, from an overzealous bath. Would they put that on the death certificate? Capitalized, Death by Bed Bath. When I returned, to the nursing station, the head nurse was bent double. She said that I had so much soap on him that he looked like one big soap bubble. She advised me to limit the water and the soap. She liked me and said she would get me out of anymore bed baths. I begged off on having to do this on any future men or women.

In line with the bath failure was a prep failure with lack of soap. The middle-aged man with a hairy chest needed a chest and abdominal prep. That meant shaving of hair. The body had as much hair as a buffalo. It was going to be a large project and I had a co-worker. We found that the hair shaved easier cutting it dry. Slice and dice. I suggested using four-inch-wide paper tape to remove it. We commenced to shave the majority of a man's frontal body with disposable razors traveling at high speed. We were done in no time. There were no visible nicks or scrapes. It looked great. The perfect cut. He was happy, momentarily. The wide paper tape removed it from the body leaving clean, white skin. We wished him luck with his chest procedure and said "Good night."

A few days later, the head nurse asked, "What in

the world did you and the other orderly do to that man's chest?" "It was the worst case of prickly heat and rash that the surgeon had ever seen." —""The doctor almost cancelled the case, but proceeded, and then days later it looked worse before it got better." "He said the whole front of the man's body had ~~razer~~ razor burn." "Fortunately, he is on a surgical floor now and we don't have to see him." I was forced to explain that we tried a new technique, that we had used dry ~~raisers~~ razors and no soap. She was flabbergasted and said to never do that again. Sometimes the perfect cut doesn't last.

THE DOUBLE

"Give a woman an enema?" I gasped. "Yes." she said. "There is nobody else to do it," "and I don't care what hospital protocol is." She followed her order with a string of expletives that indicated she was tired and the hospital understaffed and her whole world was one problem after another. I was both mortified, astounded and terrified. I was barely out of my teens, still had acne, and had already done one catheter insertion that defied anatomy and was a failure. It was on a dried up, screaming female kicking like an NFL player, 90 years of age. She landed a few blows to my head. As nurse instructed, I was trying to insert a foot of urinary catheter into parts unknown. Anatomy does not look in real life like it looks on a hospital training handout. It was a mission failure, and I gave the tubing to the charge nurse to my right and left the room. There again, it was against hospital policy for men to catheterize women. Doesn't anybody follow the rules around here? Rules are broken when institutions are short staffed.

I was on 11-7 and I watched the clock all night. The enema turned out to be two enemas, and it was two women in the same room. Very bizarre, as far as I was concerned. This was another reason for my sweating and tachycardia. I tolerated my nerves till 6 AM. In a haste, I gathered the supplies and entered the room an hour early. I flipped the switch and darkness disappeared, leaving two middle aged women batting their eyes in astonishment.

"I am assigned to give an enema to each of you, and I will start with you.", pointing at the wide-eyed white female in Bed A. I rapidly infiltrated the mixture and sent her to the bathroom. Another 3 H down the pipes. I cleaned up the debris quickly and administered to Bed B. I had a great feeling of accomplishment and finality as I said, "I'm done, you can go to the bathroom now." She got up, turned and sputtered in horror, "She's in the bathroom." She said it loud enough to be heard in the hall.

Oh my, what a mistake I had made. This will cost me my job. I was sure. I had never done a double before in the same room. How was I supposed to remember that the rooms only had one bathroom?

It was never an issue. I was speechless, unable to even think. The silence was deafening for about 5 seconds till what neurons I had at age 21 took over. Everything suddenly registered with me, including what a fool I was. The rooms had one bathroom and there was another hundreds of feet down the hall.

I said the only words I could say. "You will have to go down the hall "

The last I saw of her; she had yelped and was sprinting down the hall like Zorro in a cape. The entire gown, tied at the neck was waving behind her as she struggled to hold the back together. She disappeared behind a single door at the end of the hall. As she leaped by an open waiting room, visitors caught a glimpse of a blurred white figure in a gallop, cape flowing.

When I saw all of this unfold from her doorway, the whole sorry encounter came together. I had to cover my mouth as I went into paroxysmal spasms of laughter which I couldn't release. I laid against the wall with my back and bent double as the spasms regressed. Bed A was still in the bathroom. I bolted and with a straight face returned to the station with no semblance of any of the difficulties. No inquiry was ever done. I had vanished into the system again. Thank goodness.

THE WRONG FUNERAL HOME

"Call the funeral home on 204, she is dead." Said the nurse. "Then, I will show you the protocol." This was a mission that I had never been on. I had never called a funeral home for anything. I never had thought about a funeral home even having a telephone. Dead people tell no tales, at least that's what I had heard. I was efficient, however and I seized on the moment with great joy, at having the trust and responsibility. I grabbed the phone book, selecting a half page advertisement that appeared to be fine and upstanding. I made the call. I laid out the problem. They advised that they would be right over. Quickly, they showed up, looking the part, tall dark suited men rolling a gurney down the long hall with anticipation. The nurse looked down the hall and looked from me to them in spurts of interest and curiosity. I knew that something was amiss. She finally yelled, "Where did you get the number?" I said, "The phone book." She grunted, gasped and said, "The number was in the chart, you called the wrong funeral home." I was aghast. How could you call the wrong home, didn't they all do the same service. How hard could it be?

Then the nurse explained one of the most bizarre things that I had learned in my tenure. "The funeral home number is in the chart.", she said. It was entered at admission. I was shocked. I thought, In the chart, the patient's chart? Like you come into the hospital and pick an embalmer, in case things don't go as planned. I couldn't believe it. She had to send the two anxious funeral directors out the door, sad and downtrodden, pushing the stretcher in long strides, no conversation.

The two men put up no protest, demanded no retributions. I disappeared around the corner and listened to more of the exchange. "The new hire called you by mistake, ", she explained. I cringed. Would this go in some report that would speak of me as the incompetent orderly, who couldn't even make a phone call. Maybe I had been discovered. Then, I relaxed, this was probably the least of what they thought I did not know.

After they left, the nurse said, "Put plastic over the body and straighten the room." I complied and found myself in the room with a dead body. I moved slowly and quietly around the aged corpse. I sensed a need to show respect. In addition, I was scared senseless. I straightened the room, and saw the wrist lying there, motionless. I reached over and took the pulse, it was thready. I became alarmed. Was the woman dead? Then it would stop and be thready again. I took off to the nursing station and grabbed the nurse and advised her to come with me. She took the pulse; it was very sporadic and faint. She advised that this was electrical activity that would not support the heart, and this was not a heartbeat. I relaxed. The activity stopped. Plastic wrap was placed over the body and I left the room.

Years later, in another hospital, in yet another job while I was in college, I was on midnight shift. I was advised, by the regulars, that if you dared, you could catch an hour or two of sleep in the morgue, down some long stairs to a landing. It was a quiet respite, in a long shift. This was done between 2 and 4 o'clock in the morning. I did not participate. I assumed I would be the one caught and fired.

What later happened to an employee cast aspersion on any further sleep on that shift. The proposed sleeper pulled a stretcher up, from the other end of the room to the stairwell, and went safely to sleep. As he slept, an employee was sent to the morgue. When the employee reached the bottom of the stairs in the dimly lit room, he found an assumed body under a sheet, head covered, blocking his access. The employee grasped the end of the stretcher and pushed it handily out of the way. The stretcher blasted into a wall causing the startled sleeper to raise up on his elbows and scream "What's going on down here?" This forced the employee to lunge upward on the upstairs, in fear of all that was there, jumping, cascading and not making it. He fell back down the stairs, breaking bones in his leg. This ended the exercise of rest while on the clock at the hospital. I was glad that I had not availed myself of the nap.

"That doctor is going to kill somebody." said the patient with a rotten hole in his buttock, exposing his hip socket. He blamed an old doctor. His story was about an injection in his hip that resulted in a staph infection threatening his existence. He believed the needle had not been sterilized. He was septic and sick. In those days, injection needles were not disposable. They were reused on numerous patients after sterilization procedures had been performed. In addition, since an injection is an entry into the body, an infection could result regardless. Likely, infection rates decreased, when disposable needles became standard of care. The man improved and did not die, from that.

I answered a call to a room where the patient advised me breathlessly that he was about to have a seizure. I asked, "How do you know? "With wide eyes, he said, "I know." He then went into a full blown grand mal seizure with the bed shaking as if it would turn over. I got help and we restrained him until it was over. A seizure of that magnitude can break bones in legs and arms. It was an upsetting sight. It was more disturbing because I found that patients can become aware of an oncoming seizure. The brain is giving a warning. Trouble is coming, take cover.

CALLED TO PRONOUNCE

The thick chart was held together by a wide rubber band, bulging, and in a stack on the nursing counter. The stack was labeled "to medical records". The patients were either dead or discharged and no longer in the facility. I removed the top chart and disassembled it. The last progress note read in scrawled print, "Called to Pronounce", the letters capitalized, as if to grab attention or prominence. It appeared the patient had died alone.

I dug in. The doctor had responded to the bedside for a request. He was fulfilling hospital protocol. The doctor knew nothing of the patient other than what was recorded. The patient had no regular doctor. He was admitted to the hospital service. Hospital policy demanded a pronouncement of death prior to removal of the body from the hospital. The nurse announced a need, a doctor responded. The nurse could not pronounce the patient dead. That was a doctor's responsibility.

I wondered, as I read the entry. Is this what life

degenerates to? To be declared dead by an unknown doctor specifically sent to the bedside for that purpose. Perhaps, the doctor was exercising one last demand prior to his return home. He had worked all day; this was his last responsibility. It was a job that I am sure he was not fond of. Basically, he declared the man dead and then the other hospital rules took over on departure. A quick task, as he ran out the door. Rules. Signatures. The charting of failed vital signs. The call to the funeral home. The unclaimed body. The burial in a potter's field.

The patient was going the way of all the earth as the Old Testament stated. The mortal end had come. I wondered how he died, I read on. Heart failure. Nice descriptive term for the end of life. You don't live long if the heart decides not to. It just seemed so terminal and sad. Empathy rose up. There was nothing I could do, no one to console. I guess what bothered me was the "alone" segment of the death. Dying alone, with an unknown doctor combined with "called to pronounce" completed the picture. I thought about becoming a forest ranger. I loved pine trees. Maybe, I should run from healthcare.

SAVED BY AN ADMISSION

She was murdered September 26, 1974, in her stately home in Searcy, Arkansas. Her name was Fern Cowen Rodgers, wife of renown physician, Dr. Porter Rodgers, Sr. M.D. I received the news in Chicago. I sat down feeling weak and sick. My head was spinning. A stack of newspapers with the account accompanied the horrific news. I was stunned and replayed the whole relationship in my mind from months earlier. I closed my eyes; I didn't want any interference. I wanted an accurate review.

It was the Spring of 1974, four months earlier. The antebellum mansion was a southern beauty. It sat on Race Street in Searcy, Arkansas, the main drag, as we called a busy boulevard in southern towns. I peered through the landscaped front yard at a two-car garage with a garbage apartment over it. The entire yard was picturesque. Very southern. Very perfect. I was tired of the dorm. This place was walking distance to the college. Rules allowed a senior to live off campus, generally married. I would have that designation the next year. I was ready to move into my own place. I don't why. I had no furniture or possessions. As in youth, many ideas are fraught with foolishness, leaving one to wonder later, "Why did I do that?"

As was my custom, with no consideration of disturbing the home owner, I knocked loudly on the door. With that movement of my knock, I entered a part of my life that has spawned more questions than answers. I have never been comfortable in telling and retelling the events of that next few months. Now, with this news, it had raised spiritual questions on the intervention of God in my life.

A congenial, nice, older, amiable lady opened the door, with anticipation. I suspected she thought that I was a peddler selling something, that would need to be dismissed. Thoughts of my failed cookware venture returned. I introduced myself, and asked if the garage apartment was for rent. She looked curiously, and asked," How did you know about it?" She said that in a tone as if I were hiding something. I told her that I did not know about it. I had just walked by and seen it. She led me, alone, through the house, out a covered breezeway and to the stairs upward to the apartment. At the locked door, she pulled out the key, hesitated, and said in this melancholy voice, "I haven't rented it in a long time." It was like she was thinking about some event. Being an immature 21-year-old, I put no thought into her demeanor, but later thought of the voice inflection. She opened the door, slowly. It was stuck. We went up the stairs, single file, and peered at a dusty, attic looking room with a bed and other items. She said, "75 dollars a month and free first month if you clean it up." I told her that was fine and we parted. She had never given me her name.

That week, I went back to my part time job at the hospital. I told my mentor, the old nursing assistant, of the home and the apartment. She was amazed that I didn't know the home or who it belonged to. She said, "That is old Dr. Rodger's home, he owns a hospital, and you spoke with his wife." I knew the boy that lived there and worked with him the night that he died." "He had your job, here in the hospital, orderly." "He had to drive to Memphis that night, and did not want to go, said he had a bad feeling about going, he died in a car wreck." With this information, any sane person would have run from that job and the newly found living quarters. With the immaturity of youth, we just don't think.

The nursing assistant then told me a host of gossip and inuendo, the rumor mill of the medical community, prized stories, true or not, that people like to tell. They were all about his practice, wealthy life, the dropped counterfeit money charges years earlier. She knew for a "fact", that the machine was still in the basement. She told of the good job, medically, that he had done in his practice. She told the good and the bad, the gambling in Las Vegas, world class quarter horses - Carbon Copy and Rodgers Perfection at Fred Webb Stables. The lengthy tale lasted for weeks, as I was told bits and pieces every time I came to work. Information overload. In some of the recounts, there was impropriety that I wondered how she could know. I gave her great credibility, however, since she had picked out the fake doctor weeks before all the doctors and others had. The Rodgers family was so well known and prominent, it would be impossible for the masses not to tell stories and probably make up a few. Both father and son had huge practices. The son was a fine surgeon and had wonderful bedside manner. I was around him at the hospital, but never mentioned the rental relationship with his mother. He was just another good doctor and

was kind to me when I did his patient orderly tasks.
I stayed a few nights in the apartment during
March- June 1974. I would be awakened at around 5
AM, with sounds of dragging or bumping, coming
from the side entry by the garage. I finally, got up and
positioned myself, to figure it out. It was the doctor
carrying a suitcase that would scrape against the wall.
I dismissed that, as him returning from some
destination. My car was parked on the street or in the
driveway. I was never given any instruction. She was a
nice, kind, lady that I spoke with often. I told her that
I was at the hospital part time, that I wanted to be a
podiatrist. She said that she used a nice podiatrist in
Hyannis Port, Massachusetts. She never mentioned
the tenant before me, and neither did I.

My last encounter with the mansion was the middle
of June, 1974. I had left the end of May and made one
final night there in June. My parents and brother were
traveling with me. We slept in the small apartment. it
was a hot summer night. The air conditioner stopped
at 2:30 AM. The entire complex went black. without a
sound. It became hot. It was unsettling and earie. I
didn't feel right. This would later become interesting.

My mind then returned focus on the newspapers.
On September 26, 1974, Mrs. Fern Rodgers was found
dead on the stairs of the home. In a few weeks, a trio
was arrested. Dr. Rodgers Sr. along with Peggy Hale
and Berry Kimbrel, who actually fired two shots into
Fern Rodgers causing her death. Her pocketbook was
found a few feet from the garage apartment in the
yard. The investigation was immediate,
comprehensive and attracted nationwide interest.

I was now horrified and grieved, but also had a
lump in my throat, over one of my actions. I had left
the apartment the end of May, 1974, as a result of an
admission letter that I received from Illinois College

of Podiatric Medicine, beginning studies in Fall 1974. I had been in Chicago since the end of June. I was borrowing money for education and had written Mrs. Rodgers and asked if she would loan me $ 3000.00 in that endeavor. This was not good. Absolute complete immaturity on my part, at age 21. The foolishness of youth, that someone would amass money, stack it up, and give it out to the whelms and desires of ill planned schemes. I surmised that somewhere in that crime scene laid that letter, now part of an investigation. They would at least want a statement or a demand to come to Arkansas. Hopefully, Mrs. Rodgers had tossed it wisely into the garbage.

I called the FBI in Chicago and told them of the letter, the returns with the suitcase in early morning hours, my immaturity, and the recent unsubstantiated babble that I had heard at the hospital. An agent recorded what I said for over an hour. I was never recontacted. As the trial later unfolded, the gossip turned out to be completely correct, from the young girl, to the traveling to Las Vegas, living in a Searcy motel, and other parts of the case. In addition, the killer, William Berry Kimbrell, in testimony, related that the murder was planned earlier in the summer, but something came up that night. He never related what stopped the plan that night in June. I sensed that what came up that night was a strange car in the driveway, my dad's Rambler Station Wagon.

He also testified that he (Kimbrell) had been instructed to kill everybody at the house on the night of the murder. Mrs. Rodger's sister, who stayed over some, was not present that night. Neither was I, having left months earlier.

I would have been there in September had I not been accepted into the Illinois College of Podiatric

Medicine. An admission saved me. My well-being was protected. Thoughts of God were inevitable.

Trial testimony revealed a fee of $ 6000 for the murder of Fern Rodgers. The trial was huge in the state and the entire sultry, sordid, affair made the public crave every detail. Berry Kimbrell was imprisoned and died in 1992. Dr. Rodgers died in 1980, receiving a sentence of life in prison, for planning the murder of his wife. Both died serving their sentences.

CHICAGO

Chicago was a long way in culture and distance from South Georgia and Arkansas. After a few weeks living there, I decided that the prudent course would be to award anybody a degree that managed to survive living there. They had deserved it. Crime was a problem. The medical bag had to be disguised in a wrinkled sack suggestive of a homeless person. Only a fool would walk down any street in Chicago with a medical bag in hand. It would be paramount to wearing a sign that said, "I have drugs and money, come get it."

Just the sheer volume and mass of humanity was overwhelming. Everywhere one went there was a few thousand people around you. Extending your arms outward in any store, street, or building could contact another Chicago resident.

As students we parked in all manner of parking decks and a back alley, to avoid paying parking fees. Condemned buildings were prime parking locations, squatters on property that we could give a few dollars to watch our cars. We walked down the street at night in the middle of the empty streets so the street lights would illuminate any dangerous entities. A noise, a crack, a voice and we would sprint into the darkness. My African-American friend said "There was only one way in Chicago to prevent a car break-in in a bad neighborhood." "The answer was to purchase a decal from a local, traditionally black college." "Put the decal on your car, and if the perp is black, he will not break in." I was astounded but figured that it could make sense. Several students did it. I did not.

On the train leaving Chicago, to my rented apartment, south of the city, a young girl, ran in from the platform. As the double doors opened, she screamed, "Come off and help me, my boyfriend is in insulin shock." I leaped to my feet, ready to plunge into the damsel in distress situation. As I made haste to vacate, a spectacled man lowered his newspaper on the train, and said, "We are at 63rd Street, if you get off here, we will never see you again." He then stuck the newspaper back up, hiding his face, as if he had just done a public service announcement. He was very persuasive. I sat down as fast as I had leaped up. The girl begged, but I held out and said, "I'm not getting off." She ran out through the double doors exiting as they slammed shut. How do people stay alive here? I wondered. Certainly, it could be difficult for a gullible southerner not to fall for schemes. We are always taught to be helpful and kind.

The Chicago train rides from the suburbs pitted travelers against each other for good seats, clean window views, and access to the opening door. Some of the train cars were old enough to have been ridden by John Dillinger in his travels. In one trip, I noticed the same man, each day, reading a Chicago Tribune. After reading, he would methodically and precisely tear the paper into long strips stacked neatly to his side. For a week, I decided this was the behavior of a deranged psychopath. At the end of four days, having ridden across from him each morning, I realized his actions were simple. He was preventing anyone from reading his discarded newspaper. Certain attitudes and actions were incomprehensible to me, and this was one of them.

Another day, I was in a blinding snow storm poking through a neighborhood when I passed a man covered in snow, walking in the gusts. I stopped and picked him up. I was in a Volkswagen which placed us close together. He leaned in, a few inches from my face and said, "You got any money." I said, "Great, so I pick you up in a snowstorm and now you rob me." "No, I have no money, I am a student." He dropped his head and said, "Sorry man, I won't rob you." I said, "Thanks." I carried him to where he was going and dropped him out. He thanked me and apologized again. Sometimes, in Chicago, you just have to beg to avoid being robbed.

I found that running away from trouble was an acceptable escape. Better a coward than a dead hero. At one point, my car died in an intersection blocking all behind me. The man behind leaped from his car, ran to mine and advised me to put it in neutral, "he would tow me." I did and he accelerated. At 60 miles an hour, with the man on my bumper, I found an opening and made it to the opposite shoulder. He pulled up behind me, got out, and said, "I want twenty-five dollars for towing you out of that intersection." I nodded in agreement, exited my car. I then ran, darting through a neighborhood, hiding behind a house. I peeked out. He threw up his hands and left. I approached my car and left as fast as I could. In Chicago, I found that sometimes you have to run to stay alive.

NO SUDS

The shampoo warehouse in Chicago was four miles from the apartment. It was separated by scads of tiny houses on small lots with tree lined streets with cars that lined the sidewalks. It was like a stationary motorcade welcoming you to the neighborhood. I rode my bicycle through Phenix, a quiet alcove in an area of Chicago of which I knew nothing but the sign, which heralded, Welcome to Phenix.   It was dark at 5:30 AM, I saw no movement, no pedestrians, and limited moving cars in the neighborhoods. I flew along anxious on my first day of work to arrive early and show interest in whatever about shampoo and feminine hygiene products that you could get interested in. The combination of this commerce was indeed unusual. It was my summer job prior to starting the studies in Illinois.

I arrived and took position with the other new hires, many not speaking English, staring at me curiously with my southern accent and my Schwinn bicycle parked at the door. We received our gloves, towels and bottles and began working. We were advised that the products were 2, shampoo on one line and feminine cream on another. I was in the shampoo assembly line, which Henry Ford had initiated making numerous automobiles in one swoop, which meant for me, a long line of boys holding bottles under pipes shooting out shampoo. A fellow worker said "It won't lather." He related that last week, he had stolen a gallon and taken it home, eager to clear his body of the grime and dirt from a hot warehouse. Much to his disappointment, the bubbles in the shower spawned by the shampoo were little and less than a bar of soap. He had to resort to an old bar of Ivory to lather up and be cleansed of his grime. "Not worth stealing," he said as he capped the hundredth bottle of the day. It was monstrously hot in the warehouse and I knew I might not last. It was a sweat shop. Initially, I persevered.

The workday disappeared and I began my ride on the bicycle back through Phenix in broad daylight. Parts of the ride, in the light, appeared sketchy. Old houses were unkempt, with large sagging porches across the front. I pedaled and heard loud words coming from an approaching porch. Who could he be cursing at? I her; surmised that I was about to witness a neighborhood brawl between porches. Then it was apparent, as I closed in on the home, the profanity was directed at me. The young man was standing on the porch screaming, "Don't you know there are no white folks in Phenix?"

He was yelling at me, continuous obscenities and profanities that increased in volume as I gathered speed to pass the house. I sensed disaster and pedaled as fast as humanly possible. Schwinn appeared to be winning but he was exiting the porch too quickly. It was going to be an intersection of me and a madman. He reached the street and lunged full throttle at me, expecting to grasp the handlebars and catapult me off into the pavement. He missed me by one rotation of the tire and fell behind me in the dirt. My adrenal gland had kicked in and the Schwinn was traveling close to the speed of sound. I was pumping to save my life. I never slowed. Out of breath, I flew into my apartment. I never did that again. I told the story to a local the next day at work. He said "you never go through there unless you are in a car." "I know," I said.

The second day was also eventful. I was assigned to the hygiene line, the tubes bumped by with sporadic stops and starts as we lined them up under spouts. By mid-morning there was the sound of a sputter This was coming from the huge mother ship of cream above us. It was in a large shiny metal vat. This was followed by a loud boom from the container, which rained cream down on all of us, covering our heads. It was too much to wipe up, we used scoops to fling it from our heads back into the huge chrome pot, from whence it came. Then we cleaned our faces up and resumed the assembly line work. I lasted a few days, and then was back as an orderly in a facility.

HYPERTHERMIA

In 1942, he was imprisoned in a German concentration camp for Jews. He was taken outside in freezing weather and strapped like an animal into the deep snow, his eyes wide with fear. He writhed in pain and lost consciousness after hours of hyperthermia. Convulsing as they all did, somehow, he survived. It was he, that I became familiar with in a facility, thirty years after his torture. I saw the effects and watched him walk with a festinate, non-propulsive gait, ambling along, his mind somewhere behind him, going nowhere fast and finding nothing. He walked in an unfamiliar place, both physically and mentally. He was between dark and blurry. He was unsteady, aphasic, and could not communicate other than with a mumble, his motor skills having been tortured by a madman, Adolph Hitler. He seemed past the point of comfort. The medical community was outside the scope of comfort or other notions of a life well lived. His lips mouthed some creative lisp, his cheek twitching like a trigeminal neuralgia, held captive by scarred myelin sheaths on the nerves from hours of subzero temperature.

The nurse told me, "Go read his chart.", "you need to read the history." I settled into a hard chair in the corner and held the cold metal chart in my hand. All things medical were cold in the mid 1970's, chairs, walls, charts, bedpans, food, even the air. All was done in an attempt to kill bacteria and viruses, wiping all objects carefully with alcohol prior to the cold temperatures. It is postulated that cold air keeps bacteria at bay, a worthy goal for a medical facility or operating room.

In crisp black font, I read his living obituary of acts performed on him by fellow human beings. I read and read some more. It was brief, yet deep and long. How can you properly record a grotesque, horrific, experiment on living souls. With the goal of helping Nazis, Hitler used science to kill Jews with his intent to help his soldiers survive the frigid weather, the elimination of the Jewish race was the other motive. He took humans, made in the image of God and used his warped, twisted mind on their bodies, as if he had created them himself, as if he was God working on his own science project. Like a potter with clay, oblivious to the devil that he was, he molded and deformed them, He shot and gassed most. This was the function of the Jewish concentration camps.

I closed the chart, an altered person. It's one thing to study World War 2 in college, another to see the fruits of Hitler's labors. The patient was a victim of the man read about in the black and white textbooks, a shock of hair hanging like a noose across his forehead, people raising their arms in adulation, and shouting, Heil, which now seemed to be a praise of Hell. Somehow, a sharp fragment of World War 2 had stabbed me unannounced. The thoughts clung to me, on the train riding home from work. Thoughts diminished, and I cranked back up to enter work the next day.

In the South, we were taught to be kind to animals and humans. I could not imagine this barbaric treatment to even a mule, an animal prone to discipline to keep his big hooves in line in the cornfield. It was beyond comprehension to imagine a person made in the image of God, to be subjected to that. It was so intolerable that I could not imagine God allowing it. There was no rational explanation. How can you relegate stories of evil to a compartment of the brain, keeping it like a collection of arrowheads gleamed on the farm—? I decided to excise it. I resolved not to think about it or ponder on it.

In the next few weeks, I did what I had to do. I quit with no notice. I had no desire to explain my rationalization. Sometimes, in life, there is nothing to do but leave. Candidly, an old preacher had told me that unusual explanation, after he had left a ministry at a church.

It was the only job in my life that I left with no notice, no call, no contact. They eventually called me, for an address to mail the check. I didn't offer an explanation. What was the benefit of engaging in a conversation about theology, kind deeds, and the problem of evil and suffering. Books had been written about it for a thousand years. I could add little. I had no recipe or formula. I quit.

Perhaps Hitler's Hell will not be fire and brimstone, but a freezer, with the numbness and convulsions of hyperthermia, to torment him into all eternity.

MY DEAD BODY

With trepidation, I gazed down on my own dead body, the one that was assigned to me in anatomy lab. It was a large white female. I blocked out thoughts of exactly what this was, instead considering it as a model. It was rubbery from the formalin. My thoughts hit reality. This mental position did not last. I realized a faded armband was on the wrist. Suddenly this became personal. I surmised it was an identification for the company or lab, but, no, this was an actual faded hospital armband. I was mortified. The name could be read with close inspection. I shrieked for the lab guy to come over. The professor explained that the body was unclaimed and donated by the hospital to medical schools. Having been processed by a private company and hung in formalin for six months, it was ready to be dissected. However, he did admit that it was certainly a violation at some level. I felt sick. I felt sicker when I got home that night and the first name was mentioned on a television show related to one of the characters. I had to wonder how much of a circumstance this was. It was a little too coincidental, but I did not dwell on it. Some things have to be filed away.

I entered the lab the next day, always in a basement, who knows why? It's dark, the light is turned on, the instructor makes some cad comment, "~~you~~ You never know what's walking around down here." "A fog of formalin hits you full force. You don't have to wear a mask, but the mask seems to dull the odor. I pushed her name in the back of my mind and forged on. We wore gloves for a few weeks, some chose not to, after getting use to the rubbery feel. It did not feel like anything that had ever been alive.

In Anatomy class, we had to purchase the skeleton of a human leg. This was real. The bones were held together by metal wiring. This was 1974, purchased initially from India. It was retrieved from a beach and sanitized and sold to schools in the United States. It was real and all parts of the bone, foramen, lumps and bumps on the bones with long names had to be labeled and studied. We carried these back and forth to the school. However, Cadaver specimens could not travel out of the building.

In this case, I had the whole body and it could not be studied but in the lab hours. A skinny cadaver was more expensive than an overweight one. The structures for learning were more easily identified on a skinny person. Adipose tissue made the search for nerves and vessels harder. Schools had to pay a processing company for the bodies. The entire cadaver was studied followed in the next semester with a leg. We each were given a leg that also could not leave the lab. It could only be studied there in the basement. It was from hip down.

One student, incensed over this rule, insisted that

he needed more than 9 hours a week learning the leg. He hatched a plan and located an extra leg in the lab, stole the leg, carrying it home in an old briefcase. He kept it through the semester on the bottom shelf of his refrigerator, below the potato salad, studying it at will, on his terms. He passed the course and did very well on the examinations. I envied him but had no fortitude to steal a leg. My search for academic achievement only went so far. I had limits.

At the end of the semester, the next problem arose, as to how to dispose of the leg. He was not willing to dispose in household refuse. He speculated that it could be traced by neighborhood garbage. I heard later he had folded the leg into a briefcase and left it in a train station in Chicago. I heard no substantiation as to the validity of this tale. I was certain this was against the law and could result in his removal from the school or shot with a firing squad. I dismissed it from my thoughts, I did not want to know and it was too much to waste my neurons on.

Previously lived manner of life hurls to a stop in professional school. It is a cramming of information of gargantuan proportions. There is no time to learn of current songs, fads or cars. The band, "Lynyrd Skynyrd"the crashed in 1977. The lead singer and others died in the plane crash. They were icons, but we were in professional school and could not mourn.

You are literally dropped out of the world into another universe for years. Friends in the universe come and go. There is no time for nurturing. Richard Nixon was resigning on television, August 8, 1974. I caught it for mere moments and then resumed studies. It was unimportant in what I was attempting to accomplish. Obviously, interpersonal relationships and marriages suffer immensely in this pressured atmosphere of academia. You enter thinking anatomy is hard, then you realize you have another five classes of equal difficulty.

In the four years of study, I did not see Illicit drugs, except for one, uppers. These were tiny white pills sold by the name of "white cross." They circulated toward the last two years around exam time. They were taken infrequently and sporadically by students. After listening for a couple of years, as students espoused it as equal to a few cups of coffee, I took one, for one test, anatomy. It was free since I didn't buy a whole bottle. I never took another, as I had reservations about any drug, including alcohol, nicotine and caffeine.

It caused a 48-hour non- sleep interval. In the first part of that interval, 6 hours of study resulted in a photographic memory of entire pages. In the second part, day of exam, entire content was recalled. I made five hours of A in Anatomy that semester. The crash was evening of the second day. Bedridden in a stupor for 12 hours. You wondered when you awoke if you could recall anything, or tell a spleen from a liver. Then, good as new, An A posted on the board. I didn't want to do that again. There was a feeling that something was outside of your control. At some point of use, you could be addicted. I declined further offers and kept my head in the book and avoided chemicals.

WE ENTER THE SANCTUM

The man in starched operating room attire entered, as we crowded together across the room. This was the inner sanctum. The source of cures and curses. The operating room. The little man with a starched costume appeared to be the surgeon, in a little early. Students were early as well.

The patient was not in the room. We initiated conversation, as he checked some machine on the end of the table. We were impressed. Our first doctor contact, nice and talkative. We relaxed. Who said doctors were prideful jerks? This guy was great. He was clothed in the rich attire of an operating room surgeon. Cool as a cucumber.

He was talkative, nothing about medicine or why we were there, only small talk. Then he left. After the surgery had started, he entered again and began wiping the wall and some blood from a section of floor. He was in housekeeping. We looked at each other silently. We missed the diagnosis on that one. I wondered if anybody could just walk into a hospital with scrubs on and start work. Who would know? I learned later, that doctors rarely wore starched scrubs, theirs were battle stained and faded. Mark of the trade. A sign of years of work. No fashion statements.

The patient rolled in on the gurney, obese, 350-pound female. Legs spread, the prep was done for a dilatation and curettage of the uterus, a D and C. The anesthetic was general and the patient was sedated. We were externs, in for observation on a general surgery rotation.

The doctor was at the foot of the table standing between large heavy separated legs. He picked up a curette and turned to us, "Crowd around," he said. About five of us were there. Nobody said a word. We were all told that any single word would expel you from the OR. Doctors are not spoken to on rotation, unless they initiate the conversation. We were told not to talk if there was a doctor in the room. Nurses and staff were fine, no doctor. We were silent, eyes wide. I did not know three of the five faces. We had all prepped and scrubbed and had on surgical gloves. No one said a word.

He held the instrument up and pointed at us in a group, then singled me out, and said, "Today, you are doing this D and C." I was flabbergasted and felt light-headed. I nodded and stepped forward as if I was eager to fulfill the request. How could I refuse an attending? The realization from orderly days hit me. Here again, I know nothing.

He placed a curette in my palm and laid out several on the sterile table. He said, "You enter gently with the curette at the positions on a clock." "Like, start at 12, then do 2, then 4, then six and so forth, like a clock running clockwise." "Bloody tissue will come out, this is normal." "Continue pulling out with a sturdy grip, not a hard push, until I tell you to stop." He was beside me directing, he did something additional as I watched. Finally, in what seemed like an eternity, he said, "That's enough." Blood and corruption dripped on my shoe covers. He began some sort of bandaging, as I watched. I appeared cool and collected. Inside I was wondering how big an infraction this would be. I assumed I was operating under his supervision. He said something to me about "dictating the operative record." At that point, A tall, gentleman stepped forward addressing the surgeon, "He, nodding at me, said, in a quiet, subdued voice, "He is a podiatry student on rotation here." The surgeon shrugged, "I thought he was a third-year general surgical resident like you." We all left the room. I exited down another set of stairs seeking solace and solitude.

The word spread quickly on the campus, a student, first day, had done a D and C, while the surgical residents watched. It was a good story and gave me credibility. One for the South.

My fame was short lived. I was placed the next week scrubbed and retracting with an army navy retractor inside an obese female for a cholecystectomy, the removal of the gall bladder. The surgeon announced that she was "fat, female, fertile and forty", apparently, the classic triad for a nonfunctioning gall bladder. The room was hotter than a South Georgia tobacco field. The air was non circulating. We sweated. The time grew tense. The gall bladder was not easily identified. It's not like a picture book where pages were found and removed. The first hour, I decided this work was awful. I would rather dig a ditch. The second hour, I decided that I would never do this for a living. Into the third, I perspired profusely and dropped sweat off my forehead into the operative draped field and the open abdomen. I was struggling holding an army navy retractor attempting to expose the pit that contained grappling hands. My fingers burned and hurt. The surgeon said, "~~you're~~ You're out~~."~~—!", as if I were being removed from a basketball game and the coach was eliminating the failures. I burst out of the operating room and found a lounge where I decompressed by staying in a corner to avoid questions. No complaint was filed by the surgeon. He had more to worry about than a sweaty student. He was perspiring as well, just didn't drip into the wound. A nurse informed me that copious irrigation was done and the patient did well.

As it turned out, we were used in all manner of procedures in the rotations, scrubbing on multiple cases and seeing every disease known to man and unknown to us.

INFORMATION OVERLOAD

Massive amounts of information were coming at us. It was overwhelming. The medical language itself presented a challenge. The courses were tons of reading and memory. Then, the hospital rotations started throughout Chicago. Students in costume, the scrubs, top and bottom, provided the access. A name badge completed it. Gone were the white pants and white shirt of orderly days in the South.

We were thrown into operating rooms as bystanders, cheap scrub labor, and along the corridors and halls of big institutions. We were throughout the Emergency Room. We were bottle eyed and observing. We were in groups of students that included medical residents. It was fast paced and never slowed. We were asked questions by attendings either to teach us or embarrass us, it depending on the bold dry humor of the questioner.

We were exposed to attending doctors in varying decades of life. Some had made it, others seemed to be struggling. You would hear of some dude's third or fourth wife. One doctor said, "Some nurses are looking for the MRS degree." Acronyms were common, it was almost like a slang code among spies in a hidden medical facility.

Gomers had been a term for years describing an older patient with a chronic condition that never seemed to improve. Add a few unbathed days, the unwashed clothes and you completed the picture. You generally had an entire emergency waiting room full of them, all glaring through at the open hallway, demanding an immediate access. Years later, someone coined the meaning. Get Out of My Emergency Room. A GOMER. Others said it was, "Grand Old Man of the Emergency Room."

The O sign, a deceased person with the mouth wide open, eyes open or closed. The Q sign had the tongue slid to one side or the other. Sometimes we initiated our own codes. AGD, Almost Graveyard Dead depending on falling vital signs. "Do Not Resuscitate" was written and taped on the front of a few charts. At first glance, I thought it betrayed the Hippocratic Oath, but came to realize there are some conditions that keep us alive but are worse than dying.

It was not uncommon for an overzealous author to leave a mark on a chart depicting the quality or status of the patient. Many charts had hand-written notations clearly visible for others to read. Gomer had been seen, as well as scrawled illegible "chicken scratching" as my fifth-grade teacher would call it in writing class. These aberrant abbreviations would have been cause for lawsuits if the chart was sent out as a copy to some request that went awry.

I came to hypothesize that the exposure of doctors and nurses to abject grief, sickness, sorrow and distress was too much for mortals to bear. I wondered if I should have been a forest ranger. Health care workers tolerated it in various ways. Dry humor, nervous laughter, escapades, a burdened countenance, alcohol, stoicism were a few of the varied responses. There had to be a rebuttal by the brain of some endeavor that could allow the staff to even function after a day of this. It was hard to stomach even after having been in healthcare for years.

The exposure is what is significant in the hospital. Exposure to germs from others that Louis Pasteur and Alexander Fleming only dreamed about. Hundreds of people coughing and spitting in unison and rhythm was the norm.

To stagger in sick and leap out, interaction was required by a host of moving parts. Treatment must involve a standard of care. One must have the correct medicine administered with the correct name on the bottle. One needs rest, without endless sedation, unless, it is the sedation that one needs. The staff must be trained and ready to work. They must have an ounce of common sense. The bedpans long for a respectable temperature on the posterior. The patients place themselves in the care of those hired in mercenary services for the sick.

For the doctors and to some degree the nurses, it could become a "cubicle psychosis", going from one white curtained, cubicle or hospital room to another, a portion of those patients facing an end, some an eminent end, some a debilitating accident. Others, the needs seemed less apparent. A symptom required investigation, no matter how benign appearing. To blow off and disregard, a numb, burning foot could come back to haunt you two years later with a diabetic diagnosis, or worse, amyotrophic lateral sclerosis. ALS.

A mother was told that her daughter would never walk again, or a son would never come home again, or a host of other maladies that permeate the world. I asked God where he was on many occasions. I was glad that I had known God and met him, in the South, before I went North. Not that the South was any better, but that I had learned of God growing up before facing such tragedies. I had seen much distress growing up and this was a continuation, but I had some faith, at least to answer my doubts. I had a framework for working it out and building my life with a structure that would stand. I certainly faltered, but had a backdrop or a support behind me. We all did. The fire and brimstone sermons played a part, as the preachers that propagated this, also preached on the kindness and love of God. The fire just got more attention under a South Georgia sun.

Then I saw evidence of God, infinite true love, a black twenty something male, who suffered debilitating strokes and was rendered disabled and unable to speak, being comforted and visited by his parents every day in a long-term care facility. Pushing him down the aisle, knowing that God would surely let him know that they are in attendance, touching him, as parents are called to do, with this insurmountable grief. God bless him and them. I felt that God sent me those incidents for a reason.

The disabled white male who did motorcycle racing because he knew what was coming at age 50, Muscular Dystrophy, that had sent his father to bed as well, disabled at 50. He did 30 years of all that he wanted to do in sports, racing, and bringing life to himself, with knowledge of a dark cloud coming. Now, with legs like spindles and loss of function, he tolerated his condition with his knowledge of doing all that he could do, even as the dark specter of immobility hovered and gained a footing. He was cheerful and laid in bed knowing that he had done all that he could do. It helps to reach that point. Then we assign the remainder to our Creator.

The man who completed his crops, the goal of a harvest being realized, had the dark area on a leg examined. He speculated that it was a chronic burn resulting from resting the leg against a warm tractor part, during crop season. He learned that it was a deadly skin cancer, amelanotic melanoma, that is diagnosed late, because of the absence of pigment. The inguinal lymph nodes were positive and the patient died within two years. The doctor, having attended a dermatology seminar days earlier had recognized the presentation on the patient that afternoon and sent him straight to oncology.

The toes were cyanotic with blue dots, some kind of Walt Disney appearing creation called emboli to the toes, bits of infarcted dead tissue from blockages thrown off her heart valves from subacute bacterial endocarditis, SBE, a killer. She was surviving and she did live. We stood at bedside, five of us looking at both feet that would certainly be on future medical boards and state licensure exams. We inspected her like a bug in a microscope slide, noting the lab work in the chart, her presenting symptoms of general malaise and fever and her improvement with the correct treatment.

A perfect disease presentation is a time for learning. There is nothing better than seeing a malady outside of a textbook. A man under a white sheet with an enlarged prostate is fair game for educational endeavors. He endured four of us palpating the mass with ample supplies of jelly. We did not line up like an assembly line, but examined intermittently over a two-day period. The initial clinic doctor discovered the enlargement and passed the word, "We have an enlarged one." Amazingly, it was years before the prostate specific antigen, PSA, was discovered and made this type of exam of less importance.

One had difficulty learning on small organs, there needs to be enlargement like prostate or spleen for definitive palpation allowing us to feel the pathology. Learning was everything to everybody. One thing we learned was that you can be really sick and look really good. On television, the victim always announced his demise, "I am dying." Then he did. It was a little different in the hospital. We realized that death was something that you had to live with, and observe it as it proceeded, with its ups and downs, and final gasp. In others, it came and went as easy as a lost breath or absent quantity of blood.

An 85-year-old shriveled gypsy woman, hospitalized with chest pain, gestured with her hands, "See my lifeline." She spoke. I showed her mine, she said, "I don't have to tell you." I assumed that meant she needed money to tell me when I would die. Since I figured that she really didn't know how close she was to it, how would she know my own future? Her future looked bleak according to her records. I declined the offer.

I learned one thing in healthcare since the orderly days. We don't know the future. You are the "picture of health", we We so admirably declare. However, it depends on who is holding the camera and I guess who knows when the flash goes off.

We stood in an old operating room, it still had old windows looking out in the vicinity of an old run-down neighborhood. The operating room was old but stable. I was not scrubbed but circulating. The procedure was cosmetic surgery. I knew little about breasts. Certainly, I did not understand the idea of reduction. But it became apparent when the drape was removed. The patient had implants and desired reduced volume. I concurred that it was probably needed, but didn't say a word. I knew better. A puncture was made, the mass was exsanguinated. A smaller implant was left. It was an effort to lower the mountainous range. Apparently, it was a success.

Then, a slab of flesh midsection was excised including the navel. It was unsettling to watch. I gulped but maintained composure. I willed myself not to sweat, at any cost. I had to see this ending. I didn't want to be removed from this one. The navel was recreated with a poke and a punch and the lengthy procedure was completed. The end result actually looked great. I thought, God, let me keep what you gave me.

I scrubbed on an appendectomy and noted that the surgeon dabbed phenol on the surgical site with a cotton applicator to prevent regeneration of the appendix and cauterize blood loss. This was late 1970's, it is not used today. I commented to an old nurse that podiatry used phenol to cauterize the nail bed and prevent regrowth of ingrown toenails. She said, "I will tell you something later." Afterwards in private, she related a story that she had heard of medical disaster. On a routine appendectomy, the tray was bumped and the entire shot glass type cup of phenol was spilled into the abdomen. It was immediately flushed but the damage was done. Quick and immediately, the patient was doomed. Peritonitis set in. I was horrified by this recounting.

I scrubbed and assisted on a routine herniorrhaphy, a repair of a man's hernia. As the doctor peered into the surgical site, he found a sticky, gelatinous cyst in the inguinal area and gravely announced, "this could be a cancer." He sent it to pathology immediately. I never heard the outcome.

My mind wandered to this occurrence when I was diagnosed with appendix cancer, thirty years later, gelatinous cysts surrounding the appendix.

A young girl became acutely ill and was admitted with fever, chills and appeared septic. She was very sick and incoherent. The condition worsened and she died in a few days. Autopsy was performed and found that she had died of lockjaw, a condition caused by the toxin produced by clostridium tetani, the bacteria that causes lockjaw. She had contracted tetanus. She had the evident contractures and spasms at time of death.

In family questioning, it was learned that she had an ear piercing a few weeks prior. Could that metal exposure have infected her with lockjaw? Possibly. Her tetanus immunization records were spotty. There are case studies found that substantiate this. Some of the older ways to pierce ears were with an air type gun that has been found, in some products, to be difficult to sterilize between uses. As in most infections, there is no definite answer as to how the patient contracted it. It is not likely to happen in any event, if the person has been vaccinated for tetanus. If that were the origin, a vaccination would have likely prevented it.

The taking of exams was a highly stressful period. Some students were hyperactive, pedantic, first row occupants, hanging on to every instruction, as if life depended on it. We called those students, "gunners" as we had in undergraduate studies. The mental image of a soldier, in a fox hole, raising up to fire erratically was not far off mark.

Results of educational failure would be devastating. Many owed large educational loans and failure left no way to pay them back. For most, passing became an obsession at any costs. Any scrap of paper that was found with questions was suspected as being an old test that had somehow surfaced. A student with an affinity for secretaries at typewriters carried typewriter ribbon in his pocket. If he caught an empty office, with a typewriter, he immediately swapped out the ribbon and put his friends on a copy project, as word for word was translated off the ribbon. It took hours and mostly revealed dull correspondence. None the less, occasionally, a series of exam questions would circulate and provide some degree of study. No one knew for sure, but grasping at straws was feasible. School was a death march, failure was run from, at all costs.

It was in this climate that my friend and I, fabricated an impossible test with unanswerable questions. It looked authentic. We left it in a copier, as if the original, had been hastily left in a dash off with test copies. We watched as groups tried to answer the questions. One intellectual announced that he thought the project was a fake test. Others disagreed. It was biochemistry and no one could agree on anything. Pandemonium reigned for a few days until the scheduled test was given and it was then evident that the found exam was bogus. There was cursing and gnashing but we never admitted to our little joke. The joy of watching the hysterical struggle was overwhelming. We found peace with humor for a few days, basking in our delinquency.

THE DRAKE HOTEL

The hardest decision I ever faced was to give up the part time orderly job, guaranteed three bucks an hour, for a new frontier. I was persuaded, amid dreams of cash, to become a bellman at the Drake Hotel, off the Miracle Mile, in downtown Chicago. It was scary because the pay was 75 cents an hour plus the tips. However, the gratuities could be substantial.

This was the late 1970's. I was hired with another costume including a red vests vest and black pants. I was lured by my friend, Jack, who bragged of one-hundred-dollar days, leaving work with a pocket full of cash. I was hooked, hired, and gone from the part time job at the hospital as fast as you could say "terminal illness."

I had accepted the hotel job after a depressing event at the hospital. I was only an orderly, certainly not trained in a Code, as we called it, and someone was dying of a myocardial infarction, a heart attack, on a weekend. I found myself pounding on the chest of a middle-aged man admitted with heart issues. He was not in telemetry or the ICU, but on the medical floor. He was not thought to be critical, until he died. Unfortunately, this is the case of many. No crystal balls around that were reliable. There was a doctor running the code, and myself pounding the chest and nurses administering medications. The patient was flat lining and was shot with epinephrine.

Then, as I pounded in some fashion, the patient experienced copious amounts of projectile vomiting, possibly from my pounding, but who knows. It covered his torso and the rest on me. Then he was pounced dead and the code ended. I was shaken mentally, and also felt some responsibility for the sad ending, though I knew that we had done all that could be done. Sometimes pounded hearts do not crank back up. The whole event was a mess in my brain.

A letter came a few days later from hierarchy in the hospital. It was an appreciative letter for actions I had taken two weeks earlier, mopping up water in an electrical area of the hospital, "above and beyond the call of duty." I had to laugh at the irony. I was congratulated on mopping a floor but still felt that I had failed my chest compressions. I was happy to start a new part time venture outside of healthcare. I was exposed to enough of that in the College.

The Drake was opened in 1920 at the corner of Lake Shore Drive, Chicago. It became famous and the place to stay. A host of dignitaries and political figures continually stayed there. In 1952, Joe DiMaggio and his wife Marilyn Monroe carved their initials into the Cape Cod Bar. The job was spiced with interludes of the real rich and famous waltzing through the lobby followed by handlers and staff.

Walking into The Drake was like some type of dream or opulent fairy tale. High ceilings, chandeliers, broad wooden panels and crown mold. Ornate stairs were present with paintings and portraits. Uniformed employees were present for the beck and call of high paying guests. The word, "front" would resonate from the front desk, signaling a well-dressed bellman to immediately come for assistance, off his preassigned post in the lobby.

I was integrated into the Drake staff and the bellman language. The term "bellhop" and "bellboy "had been dropped from the Drake years earlier. We were bellmen. A saw buck was a ten-dollar bill, a fin was a five and a C note was one hundred dollars. The best tippers were manufacturing magnates, the original founders of the companies, not the less inclined children of substance. The founders, the ones that had clawed their way to the top were sympathetic to those of us who were at the bottom of the ladder. The basic servant. They had been there. They knew we could rise above our circumstances with luck and hard work. They were especially sympathetic when I related that I was a student, which I certainly revealed in an effort to gain affections which translated at times into dollars.

I was offered a shoe shining job in between my work carrying luggage on check out and check in. I accepted and I thought it was incredible money, five to ten dollars for shining a pair of shoes. These were done after having been picked up from the room, in between the other work. I found space for my supplies and work in a basement room. None of the shoes looked as if they had ever touched dirt and were easy to look new with little effort. More money.

It was a great time to be in Chicago at The Drake because Jimmy Carter was President. I could turn on a thick southern drawl which immediately broke the ice and insured some level of gratuity. Finding out I grew up in South Georgia sealed the deal. Chicago, during the 1976 election, was mesmerized with Jimmy Carter in a campaign ad shoveling peanuts in his warehouse. It was if they had never seen a man toil. The ad blended politics, sweat, and hard work. He embodied the American dream of sweat from the brow. They appreciated his honest character and homey style. Jimmy was a hot item and never a dull topic of conversation.

Billy Carter, Jimmy's brother, was a unique individual and was watched by the media as if his comments were from the top of Mt. Sinai. He was much more astute and smarter than the media portrayed him. He stayed at the Drake promoting "Billy Beer." I loved Billy. He was one of us, a true southerner. He was friendly as southerners are, and engaging. When asked about Jimmy, Billy would speak vividly about the relationship. "You can choose your friends but not your kinfolks." The press was mesmerized and wrote down every syllable. Billy held his court in his service station in Plains and was quite poetic. This whole "Carter thing" put a lot of money in my bellman uniform. I basked and thrived in it and milked it when I was able. It was a good conversation opener on a tight elevator.

I was home and was present in the small crowd when Candidate Carter returned to Plains after securing the Democratic nomination for President in August 1976. He was driven in a pale-yellow Chrysler. I stood beside him as he addressed a nun and spoke with her about issues. I gained traction for a tip with a recounting of that story.

I knew Hugh, his cousin, in his antique shop and had met, Uncle Alton, his father's brother. I became so enthralled that I took a picture of the Welcome to Plains sign on a trip home, and combined that with a small amount of Plains dirt and sold it from the Chicago Tribune. There were a few takers. The enterprise consisted of a vial of dirt and an authenticating picture of the home of America's President, what could be better?

I never was at a loss for words, not when commerce was involved. When the elevator door closed with the guests inside, it was my cue to get busy. The elevator was my pulpit, my lectern. I had mere seconds to attach bags and suitcases to my extremities like a squid and slide myself into one elevator corner, with the family feet away. The doors closed as the employee closed them, sitting on her stool in the corner. As elevators are generally quiet, I found this to be the perfect spot to launch into a recent Chicago event, like the King Tut exhibit. The way I lectured; it sounded as if I had crawled into the crypt to retrieve him and transported him on Michigan Avenue. The goal was to extract a gratuity from their silk suited pocket to my own, all while proving useful Chicago information. I prompted conversation and dove in. I spewed verbal profusion like a leak from a cistern. I would see a sense of amusement and curiosity as I waxed on. I didn't care. I got the impression that their conception of the South was blacked out teeth and high back overalls. My persona laid that to rest. I knew enough about Chicago to impress even the most reluctant guests. I became their friend and confidant by sheer exposure. I begged for high floors, giving me more elevator time. I threw on the southern drawl and let it roll. They were intrigued to say the least.

The Drake always had a of high-ranking political figures and stars in the public arena. I served my share of them. We were assigned a post in the grandiose lobby and the order was purely a gamble as to who got what guest on a check in. The Bell Captain would call "Front" and we would rotate our turns to take each guest up the elevator. The elevator was run by a female employee with white gloves and dress heels sitting inside the elevator on a stool. It was, as we say in the South, "high cotton", a term indicating a profitable cotton crop in the season.

Goldwater visited occasionally with a cane and a limp. He was elderly by then. I believed that my father and another seven people were all that had supported Goldwater in the presidential election of 1964. My dad had been asked to leave the polls in 1964, because at 11 years old, I had an AU H2O sticker on the seat of my pants. These were symbols from the Elemental Table, the chemicals, gold and water. I was pleased that nobody knew what it meant.

I spoke with Rudolph Nureyev, the famous ballet dancer from the Soviet Union. He was lean for sure and bounced into a bus to O'Hare true to dance form.

One beer magnate tipped me well and was the reason I realized that shiny shoes made the man. I came to notice that the millionaires wore Johnston Murphy and other expensive brands. Shiny shoes meant a good tip. I noted that immediately and moved in for the kill. I was completely sincere, I just needed money to survive Chicago. There was no bait and switch, I was a good bellman and carried bags with both arms and on my back making a full display of my devotion to their business trip. I had heard stories of vindictive bellmen in other hotels, that, if tipped poorly in the room, would push the thermostat to 85 degrees on the way out. I did not schedule a 3 AM wakeup call like a dissatisfied bellboy had done in another hotel. The Drake would have been fired me on the spot if I behaved in that manner. My premise was being kind to all, and if they didn't tip, I would make it up on the next one. I left work regularly with bulging pockets of cash.

I waxed eloquent with Spiro Agnew about his visit to Harding College when I was a student, a few years earlier. He rode into Harding College in opulence as the Vice President for Richard Nixon, stepping out under sunlight in a shiny presidential suit. He gave his speech and the motorcade vanished. Later, he resigned prior to Nixon's own resignation. I complemented him on his speech years earlier. He was congenial and gave me a gratuity. I did ask and receive an autograph on the birthday card of my newborn daughter. At the college, he had come with all his glory, in a long dark limo with Secret Service bounding out and about. He left The Drake, unrecognized, with only a lone bellman asking for his autograph.

On an early morning at 7 AM, I carried Willie Mayes a newspaper and received five dollars. He was so amiable and in his pajamas. I asked for one autograph, a strict violation of Drake policy and he complied. I then asked for another, for my friend, Jack. He looked me in the eye and said, "Do you know who I am?" I said, "Yes, you are Willie Mayes the famous baseball player." His eyes twinkled, he grinned and signed another. He was a great man and a professional in his field.

Bennie Goodman, the "King of Swing" was a kind gentleman to all of us. He had grown up in Chicago and now returned to perform. He signed a card for me and gave me a five. I thanked him and he warmly smiled.

Princess Grace Kelley of Monaco came in with a huge entourage. I was asked by the bell captain to run up a delivery to her room. I was let in, and stood waiting at the doorway, while attending staff conferred. As she sat facing a mirror, I was a few feet behind her. She looked at me and smiled sweetly as the mirror reflected my own smile in return. For once, I was at a total loss for words and smitten with enchantment at the idea of receiving a smile from a real princess. She emanated a warm demeanor and I sensed that she was a kind, sweet person.

A few days later, I got Princess Grace and her entourage on a check-out. I entered the room and stacked bags and suitcases. She was beautiful. I carried a hand truck and went down the elevator alone to a fleet of limousines. I placed them in her trunk, while she gave a casual glance, looking all regal, pronouncing her approval of my handling of her bags. Her handler gave me a sawbuck, ten dollars. Not bad for a country boy from South Georgia with no royalty connections.

I got Lucile Ball and her mother on a check-out. I took the hand truck to the room. A security guard admitted me, and closed the door, while he waited in the hall. The living area of the suite was clean and empty. I said, haltingly, "Hello, is anybody here?" I was met by this voice emanating from the suite, spoken exactly like on my parents black and white television in Georgia, "Come in sonny, we are back here." I meandered through the large suite and found her and her mother in the bedroom. Her mother was a gentle sweet lady, older, short and a typical grandmother. I stacked it all up, rolled into the hall with them both, and went down the elevator. She was talkative and both had sweet smiles for me. I asked politely if she had a limo out front as sometimes the transport could be on the Walton side of the Drake. In that small elevator, she let out a huge, loud shrill, and said, "No sonny, I want you to push that cart all the way to O'Hare Airport." She shot out a laugh that deafened both me and her mother. Her mother was unfazed and I decided was used to it. I was shaken, as would be expected. I had never heard a yell that loud in an elevator. I guess she gave me the on-stage treatment.

As the door opened, she leaned down and looked directly into my face and said, "Here's something for you, don't tell my husband that I have given you a dime." She then gave me a ten-dollar bill, a sawbuck, with a spewing loud laugh. I realized then that I would soon see Desi Arnaz at the limo.

When we entered the hall, she passed a gaggle of folks, and some hollered about seeing her at the Blackstone Theater and all kinds of complements. I worked through the crowd with the hand truck and loaded the luggage in the huge trunk of a limo as her husband watched. Disappointment hit, it was not Arnaz, who had been out of the picture for years, but Dick Morton. He was nice as well, but quiet and never asked about funds given. He gave me a five and I remained silent as instructed. I opened the door for her and her mother and deposited them both safely. They waved, and rode away. Just great warm, friendly folks with no airs of superiority.

The next day, at work, I began musing about not getting an autograph from the pair. I decided I might still get one. I went to the front desk at a break and examined Lucille Ball's sign in page. There it was, nice flowing penmanship, swirls and dashes, a grandiose signature and address in Beverly Hills.

I took the risk of being fired and wrote her and asked for an autograph, advising her that I was the bellman and appreciated her tip. She sent an 8 x 10 autographed picture with a kind personal message.

An interesting side note appeared a few months later, when Prince Charles stayed at the Drake on my off days, and I did not see him. He had a visit scheduled for the Square around University of Chicago and I showed up, but was unsure exactly which side his group would pull up on.

The limo appeared in the distance, moving slowly through the traffic and stopped directly in front of me on the curb, literally 5 feet from his window. I stepped back and a security guard assisted Prince Charles from the limo, out onto the sidewalk. I realized the guard was staring at me intently and I wondered if he was about to say something. I nodded at Prince Charles and he smiled, but we never shook hands, that was off limits. We were allowed pictures.

In a minute it appeared that the guard had recognized me. Then I realized that he was a part of a security service that I had seen around the hotel. I nodded and I guess he relaxed, as his face gained some recognition.

One day, I was called over by the Bell Captain, who said, "You are checking in Oscar Meyer." I gasped, "There really is an Oscar Meyer person!" He said, "Yes, Madison, Wisconsin, the family founded the company." I was excited and I wanted that story. I was not disappointed. He was alone, a tall older gentleman, ready to talk, who was delighted in telling me of his own grandfather, the "Oscar Meyer", selling hotdogs on Clark Avenue in Chicago. The original Oscar Meyer moved from Bavaria to Chicago in 1873, starting as a butcher assistant. From humble beginnings, as an immigrant butcher, the company came to be a powerhouse. I felt as if I was in the presence of true royalty. It was a story of perseverance and hard work. It was the most compelling account of a company that I heard while at the Drake. He was a genuine aristocrat who didn't know it. He was entirely down to earth and this to me, attributed to his family's success. He also gave me a fin, five dollars for which I was grateful. The Weinermobile came to the Drake and I was privileged to see it. It stood for a fine working family who made it big in America. Here was a true story of the American dream, hard work and success. He was a most humble, kind and endearing person.

On interesting account from the 1960's, surfaced at The Drake, related to Robert Kennedy, the Attorney General, who stayed there prior to his brother, John's death. Robert gave the bellman a tip. The bellman said, "Mr. Kennedy, your brother, the President, wants to stamp out poverty and you are contributing to it." Kennedy laughed and presented the bellman with another coin.

Stories were told of new money from the currency exchange sticking to old bills quite tightly. A bellman could review his cash at the end of the day and find a hundred-dollar bill stuck tightly to a dollar. Manna from heaven.

My friend and I were on a delivery on a high floor when he turned and said, "Would you eat stolen food?" I looked curiously and said, "Maybe.", as I thought about my diet, 19 cents macaroni and cans of beans with the picture of a bean on the can. My stomach growled at the thought. My palate purred. He pointed at a set of doors leading to a storage area and said, "There is food on a server cart in there that is beyond imagination." I said, "I'm in." The waiter that had deposited it disappeared with another silver service at the end of a long hall. He would be back quickly.

Sometimes, common sense and ethics vacate the premises. Honor among thieves. We went in. There was a silver service cart with two huge trays of breakfast under large silver domes. The temptation was too great. The lust was voluminous. It embraced us. We removed all covers and it was as if a drove of locusts in Egypt during the Plagues had arrived in Chicago. We began on opposite ends and met in the middle.

The orange juice, thick with pulp, was divine. Eggs were cooked to perfection. Sausage was link and was mouthwatering. Our stomachs were on limited budgets. We were the needy that Jesus had spoken of. We were also thieves, but I omitted that from the mental exercise. The whole sordid larceny lasted less than 5 minutes. We replaced the domes and jumped a freight elevator. As we hit the ground floor running, we heard a piercing scream echoing down the elevator shaft from a waiter who had identified the loss. We hustled back to our appropriate posts in the lobby and stood whole and contented, perps with stomachs filled.

The phone at the bell captain's desk rang. We watched. He displayed a perplexed look and motioned us over. He said, "Did you see anything unusual or any strange person up on five.? After wiping our lips, we answered. "No sir." He related that the kitchen had called and said a theft of a room service tray had occurred upstairs. "No sir, we didn't see anyone." That was certainly true, the only integrity in the sorry mess. Later, I thought of the waiter, who would not get a tip because of my delinquency. The guest would get a delayed room service order. My stomach was still full, so I did not have remorse until the next day. However, the thieves did not entertain thoughts of food theft again.

Then I recalled that I had stolen food prior to this delinquency. A few times, we had stolen watermelons in South Georgia, as teenagers, initially by waltzing into the field with our knives and excising the seedless heart from the split melons. It was scrumptious. The desire was to have cold hearts of melon, after chilling in our refrigerators. We parked my friend's Ford Falcon and placed four around us in the back seat. We piled in as the farmer rounded a field curve and began chase. The Falcon took off and the driver said "Get rid of the evidence." He seemed to have knowledge of criminal activity. As we rounded dirt road curves, the car slid sideways and we tossed the melons into ditches. As the weight left the Falcon, the speed increased and we outran the rightful owner of the melons, never to go near his field again.

I checked in an elderly gentleman, and rambled on about my podiatry studies. He removed his shoe and I diagnosed his hammertoe and talked with him about conservative and surgical care. I advised him that his shoe needed to be wider, and that would probably alleviate it. I realized later, talking to the Bell Captain, that he was a renowned leader in the field of psychiatry.

Loading baggage at 7 am into a limousine at the entrance to The Drake, I observed the clock and temperature gauge on the Playboy Club across the street, in bright fluorescence, 17 below zero. As my hands turned to wooden appendages from the cold, Hugh Heffner in his black Mercedes limo rolled into the driveway. The driver opened the wide doors and Hugh waltzed out, happy as a lark, a bounce in his step, accompanied by two scantily clad playboy bunnies, obviously traveling in from the Northshore Playboy mansion. We had heard tales of the parties there. As employees of the Drake and who we came into contact with, we had received some information on those events. I thought to myself, two different pictures of life, here I am freezing a slow death, at the mercy of the tipping industry, while he is maintained by all the pleasures of Chicago. I had to admit thought, my job was better than the previous insertion of catheters and enemas. A man has to know his limitations, I guess. I waved at the bunnies and they waved back. Mr. Hefner disappeared into the Playboy Club as I pondered my job and his.

During tenure at The Drake, I was exposed to many manufacturing magnates and numerous companies founded by ones that I was serving. I made notes and tried to understand the difference between success and failure. You could say that luck was involved, but the men were all into certain attributes that were different than most. There was extreme concern for detail. Mr. Darden, founder of Red Lobster, my upper-level boss at the old Green Frog, was a micro manager that had expectations of even the position of plates and silverware as well as opinions on placemats. It seems fruitless until the originator of the micro behavior becomes world famous, then you figure there is something to detail.

President Carter was rumored to have micro managed the tennis court schedule at the White House. In a degree, this is a hallmark of success, knowing what is transpiring in the nooks of the business, though seemingly insignificant. They all had a strong work ethic, thankful for others that made them great and were positive, hardworking, people. They were eager conversationalists and shared stories and advice.

I was privileged to be the water supplier boy for a union group meeting with wage demands and benefit requests in a sequestered suite at The Drake. There were shiny shoes and slick, sharkskin suits. I had sold those suits in South Georgia delivered from Bremen, Georgia. The men were surrounding a massive table covered in papers and fountain pens, with low keyed conversation emanating from parties across from each other. Nobody was raising their voice. Details were being hammered out in unison. It was very absorbing to see the worker bargaining with the management. It gave me a visual picture of how there is an ebb and flow between the boss and hardworking employees. I was impressed with the whole affair and mesmerized as I took my time pouring water, in order to listen to the back and forth. I thought of the Vietnam War peace talks where the seating at the table had to be ironed out before talks began. This proved difficult. The Drake was a world away from South Georgia and my churched raising and I was satisfied that I had seen a part of life that I would never forget or underestimate.

HOSPITAL TRAINING

The years in professional school passed quickly. We graduated and were scattered across the country, placed in practices and residencies, never to be assembled together again. In some regard, the four years passed quickly, in others, it seemed a lifetime. There were several dropouts and marriages that did not survive the melee. How could a relationship be watered, like a plant, if you were trapped in a forest, around trees with no sunlight, or some such metaphor? They were happy until they weren't.

The amount of education seemed to be triple the amount we had been exposed to in college, and we weren't done. The massive information transfer continued into our lives in residencies combined with 80-hour work weeks and limited time off. The entire process of acceptance to the school, the education, the residencies, the cost both financially and mentally, cast its toll on marriages and relationships. The price was hard to pay for the stress and pressure that we experienced. We were in youth, so it was manageable physically, but there was emotional trauma in seeing how diseases can wreck a life and a human body.

The smells, sights and sounds of the hospital were the same. Hot sheets coming out of a dryer. Stacked blankets with an aroma. There's only one way that medicinal alcohol and healthcare smells - sterile and pure. You can package it and wrap it, but it tastes and smells the same. But this was different. Now, I was smelling it as a doctor, not an orderly, writing orders and doing the preop exams, actually, having to know what I was talking about when I opined. More responsibility, more stress, and more enjoyment. I no longer placed urinary catheters, made excuses for cold bedpans, or lied about the severity of enemas. My white outfit was complete now with a white coat. Any loss of thought that I had was covered in purity, white, and all knowledge, or so it appeared.

The young entries in hospital programs were the low hanging fruit. They were settled with long hours and trying jobs. The senior resident with his innate maturity always drove the schedule to his satisfaction. This weekend was no different. It was Christmas Day, 1979.

As the world sat down tearing gift-wrapping paper from presents and the children squealed with delight, I watched a man die. I had met him the night before, nice, kind, older gentleman. Shortness of breath escalated within his lungs becoming a full-blown cardiac arrest. Christmas day. Going to an eternal home. The code started and was run by staff, on and on, but it quickly went nowhere, fast. This patient was from out of state. He came in with minimal complaints and now he died on Christmas morning, right in the middle of the trip, miles from family. In the celebration of the incarnate God coming to earth in the form of a son, he passed from this life.

The code had unfolded with desperation, needles and jars and bottles of clear liquid and the only movement of the body was when the defibrillator shocked the chest. It raised and the flesh dropped down dead as a hammer, as we say in South Georgia. There was nothing they could do. It was his time to meet his Maker. A nurse in charge of the record wrote down all the drugs used as the code continued to no avail. She was still writing, as he lay dead, preparing his final record.

A few hours later, as the world ate Christmas dinner, the trauma continued, I watched the autopsy. Someone in the family, who couldn't fathom daddy dying on Christmas Day, demanded it. How unfair, I thought. Dead on Christmas morning. There could be nothing worse, as far as I was concerned. I watched as all the organs were removed, carefully weighed, samples taken and fluids retained. Bottles and containers held everything but his soul. It rested with God.

The life of the body flowed in a steady stream down a drain. The aroma, when the abdominal cavity was opened, was overpowering. The greasy wad placed below our noses helped block it. I watched until I exhausted my observation. I called my children in another state and asked how Christmas Day had been. The question seemed hollow as I thought about the dead man's family.

Was a doctor a prisoner of those hospital rooms? Incarcerated into a lifestyle that you can't leave, or maybe it can't leave you. Helping others is paramount. However, we all have a filing system in our minds, the neurons hide events away, catalogued so they can leap up at any time upon being summoned. You walk in, this one dies. You walk in down the hall, this one lives.

He is a GOMER, chronic illness that never improves and kills him at an old age, but only when he's ready to die. But, are we really ever ready to die? The Christian has a hope, I knew that. Other things I didn't know about.

The struggle. The loss. The gain. It was a lot of pressure per square inch. I had a thought. If the job paid minimum wage, would anybody want it? Many doctors enjoy nice things but never have the best thing-time with family or friends. That's a hot commodity. What about the pressures of breaking bad, ghastly news to families. "Your husband is dead on Christmas day." Unless one has the heartless heart, bearing that kind of news has an effect on the psyche of the bearer. There is some validity about walling off the situation and not becoming personally involved, but that is very difficult and can be considered cold. The best doctors did seem to be able to call the shots, then move on, showing empathy at the same time. One study found that a percentage of oncologists left the profession after five years. A noble calling for sure, helping people, many terminals, in this fallen world, but sometimes, unable to give everybody what ~~that~~ they wanted to hear- good news.

THE LANGUAGE OF THE SICK

There was the southern slang language as told to the doctor, from the patient, for all his maladies. Certainly, the patient was not going to call or diagnose his condition as congestive heart failure. Over the centuries it became the "dropsy.", a name for the dropped edematous fluid into the lower extremities caused by a failing heart, which was nothing more than "swollen feet." Hemorrhoids became simply "roadsroids." These were simply varicose veins of the rectum. The terms could denigrate into expressions of what was happening. Drainage became "gleet or the drip" Urinating became "making water." The patients would go to the visit with various plastic bags catching whatever was draining in an effort to show the doctor the extent of their disease. Patients carried scabs and growths in bags that had been removed by the family remedies as well as thick pieces of toenails.

Intestinal problems called gastritis could have a source in consuming yeast pills, vitamins or contaminated food after changing the babies' diapers while not washing hands. This caused diarrhea which the doctor called "loose stool." It was commonly transferred easily when handwashing was not consistent. It was called "the runs" by the patient.

Living and maintaining, the condition was described as "fair to meddling" or "vertical and taking nourishment." A familiar response from the impoverished when asked, "What are you wanting for Christmas?" was "If am just here, that will be enough."

One doctor was told, by a mentor, to never change an original diagnosis or the patient would forfeit all confidence in the practitioner and leave the practice. This doctor had told the patient that he had "locked bowels". The patient emphatically responded that it was complete diarrhea and he was unable to stop it. The pious doctor, to save face, informed the patient that "the bowels were locked wide open." This seemed to satisfy the patient who accepted the verdict. The doctor was in an "ivory tower", but could think quickly on his feet, a trait required for easy exit from a treatment room, and on to the next.

In the South, patients have taken treatment into their own hands, with remedies and potions. The Mercury head dime became a healing mechanism for the "miseries", attaching it with string to the ankle. In the patient's concept of a severe case, a double dose, one on each ankle, was needed. The Harry Truman dime would not work. It had to be the Mercury head dime with the head of the Mercury god engraved, minted in the United States, 1916-1945. As the Mercury head dime disappeared from circulation in the 70's and 80's, so did the home remedy.

The patient would not allow this to be removed for application of a dressing or cast on a foot. The dime apparatus, a dime with a tiny hole stringing it around the ankle, was covered with the wrapping as instructed by the patient. Most of these individuals were grandmothers in their 80's and 90's, having been taught the remedy by their own mother. There was no medicinal reason why this could cause anything but a reduction of disposable income, one or two less dimes to spend. These were worn for years, thought bathes, hot summers and cold winters by a segment of the Southern population who believed they had found the cure for arthritis. I saw patients weekly with the apparent lucky charm through the mid 1980' at which point they disappeared as the older patients passed away.

It was believed that dishrags were buried under the back doorstep to remove warts from the body. Walking up the steps and over the sacred dishrag would impart some type of immunity to make the warts fall off. Most warts, a viral growth called verrucae plantaris, do fall off the body with irritation so folk medicines might work in a percentage of cases. Warts are conducive to psychological or immunological disappearance, so the treatment appeared to work in some cases, only to reappear in a year resulting in a trip to the doctor.

There were the potions and recipes for wellness passed down among old family members with seemingly simple cures for various maladies. A poultice was a fabricated application wrapped on the body with many recipes. It could involve warm milk slapped on bread and then wrapped on a wound. Honey was used, aloe vera, pastes of vitamins and other recommendations from older, staid family members, who did not trust doctors. The idea of "drawing out" the miseries caused one elderly patient to wrap a poultice of extremely toxic kerosene and rags on her stasis dermatitis upon her legs. This caused ulcers to progress and she almost lost her legs as the skin came off with the dressings a week later. Upon questioning the patient reluctantly told the practitioner what she had done.

Sometimes there was a breakdown of communications from the doctor to the patient. Law requires the patient to be informed of possible drug interactions and side effects. A patient was told that the medication, "in high doses had caused cancer in rats in the laboratory." The patient appeared alarmed, but related that she would "keep the medicine on a shelf to prevent rats from getting it."

I entered the treatment room for a diabetic foot, an infected toe. The patient was in a Chicago clinic and had been using some poultice on his foot for a corn on his diabetic toe. As I entered the room, I saw the patient was missing the toe. I asked what had happened. He related it was in the bandage that he had removed and discarded in the garbage can. I retrieved the digit which was a shriveled appendage long gone, devitalized and gangrenous. The body can reject an extremity on occasion and, if cellulitis does not erupt, can cast it off like a scab with pink tissue underneath. The patient did well on oral antibiotics.

THE LANGUAGE OF THE STAFF

As healthcare and medical terminology has evolved over the years, slang terms from health care professionals have evolved as well. As medical training transformed into long years of hospital programs, the climate was ripe for an extension of the dry humor that seemed to emanate from the training. The humor was the result of hours and hours of confinement with exposure to diseases, treatments, death and mayhem. Some sayings and acronyms seemed rude, but this was not the general case and not the intention. Doctors are seeing, particularly those in the hospital as interns and residents, hundreds of patients a month. It was inevitable that some doctor or nurse on the joke spectrum would form phrases and expressions indicating the tired countenance of being thrust into a pressurized system, observing death and destruction and following endless rules and parameters of the insurance industry. It could be called the "cubicle psychosis" from entering and leaving clinic rooms and bedsides, attempting to provide healing and also explanations to the patient.

In the 1970's, as an orderly mesmerized and infatuated with reading endless charts, I saw a few acronyms for the non- compliant patient. These would be scrawled into the margins as an afterthought or taped on a chart with a small amount of tape, indicating it was not part of the medical record. These were usually by a doctor that had absorbed enough of the bedside visit to last a lifetime. In those days, records were rarely seen by others and there were no thoughts of being discovered. Most of these, sometimes coarse descriptions, were never written, only spoken in closed quarters.

After charts came to be read and studied, I noticed occasionally of an X in small letters on a face sheet or corner of a page. I asked an old nurse; she said it stood for problem patient or a general warning. Kid glove treatment written on a face sheet meant the patient was related to somebody on the hospital board.

The bedside became the key location for the nurses and doctors to deliver the care. It was the same as the cubicle of the clinic, the sacred location for good or bad news, where the doctor's demeanor was judged. The bedside visit spawned the bedside table, the prominent fake wood, squeaky, and immobile, in some cases, as the place where the enema rested or a myriad of bottles used in treatment.

I saw one description in a chart, obviously on a fake order form, "ball ping hammer to bedside." Some staff member was exhibiting final frustrations. Any of this public humor could result in a bad outcome for an employee or resident, therefore, most were never written. An attending hearing some disparaging remark about his patient could result in a severe reprimand or firing.

The list became endless as dry humorists came up with scads of abbreviations and descriptions as told by talkative dry witted doctors. In the late seventies, books were published which cemented the acronyms into the public arena, to the dismay of clinicians.

Spoken words like "pine box to bedside" or the phrase "circling the drain" indicated an eminent death. The enema was the "3 H", hot, high and a heck of a lot. MUBAR, "messed up beyond all recognition" was common. FOOBA," found on orthopedics barely alive." A "Cowboy" was the surgeon, due to ego and the rocky riding of a chain of events that sometimes follows surgical procedures. A BEEMER was a play on the body metabolic index, BMI, when the patient was obese. Zebra was the rare disease that required multiple tests. He "went south", did not mean a flight pattern.

The Emergency room had its own phrases. A Frequent Flyer was an emergency room regular. A GOMER stood for, Get Out of My Emergency Room or Grand Old Man of the Emergency Room depending on the mood of the physician. Statis asthmaticus was a medical term for asthma, Status dramatics was an offshoot which indicated the hysteria carried by some patients over any disease. FTD was "failure to die." "Conversion Hysteria" was a real diagnosis with psychiatric and neurologic overlap. The stress of the illness on the mind can cause functional symptoms of a medical nature, vague pains and unusual sensations that the mind sends down to the extremities.

A WHITE TOILET BOWL

I figured God put the clean, white, immaculate toilet bowl at the Atlanta Airport in 2001, reason being, for my hand to go plunging into it. Brand new, a label still there, I stuck my hand in the toilet water and recovered some type of tissue that had come from me. Yep, tissue, no blood. I had handled so much urine in working in hospitals that it didn't really bother me. I then scrubbed most of the epidermis off my hands at the sink and returned to the concourse. We flew on out to the Bahamas with a little of my bladder epithelial cells left in a bowl in the bathroom. I told my wife that I was melting like the wicked witch in the Wizard of Oz.

A trip to the urologist the next week resulted in a reluctant cystoscopy. The doctor admitted the incident was strange, but since I did not smoke, I would not likely have a bladder tumor, or so he postulated. I have found that most health care professionals wind up with the rarer forms of disease - just an anecdotal story, not based on anything scientific.

Yes, it was a bladder tumor, rare in a nonsmoker. The bladder was rejecting the cancer and I had seen some of it in the airport urine. The day of the biopsy came and I was admitted, biopsied for the level of cancer and discharged. Now the waiting game of the result.

I could not stand the suspense. I wanted to know; it was my bladder. What do they say? Take charge of your health. I couldn't wait for a verdict over the weekend. I did an unprofessional act. I burgled a hospital mail system and retrieved my own report before the urologist got it. The result was good. Pathology revealed no invasion, Stage 1, no need for any chemo inserted into the bladder. When he told me the next day, I never intimated that I knew already.

The urologist then hospitalized me and journeyed into the closest opening to remove the tumor. All went well. I then embarked on a cystoscopy every six months for five years. I reviewed the prognosis after surgery. Ninety percent alive after five years. I was pleased with that, but hated to be a statistic for anything.

I used to laugh at what a urologist would tell his older patients with prostate cancer. "You will be killed by some wife's jealous husband long before the prostate cancer kills you." "It's a slow grower." Remembering that, at this time, did not make me feel better, but did make me laugh again.

In the health care system, eventually, modesty is tossed out the window and you allow probing, prodding and palpating of most of your organs. It's all done in the name of living. Best done and go on to the next thing. Keep praying and move along. I was relieved in a way. I had my cancer and hopefully the statistic was satisfied and it would stop at one.

Unfortunately, a statistic is that one out of four persons who have had cancer, have another one unrelated to the first one.

I GO TO MAYO

It is 2001. I'm in Mayo Clinic with my bladder in my body and my pathology slides in my pocket. I am wishing that I could have mailed them and left my body at home. I was depressed, isolated, alone and lonely. The why me moment. Why would God interrupt my life with my health? I had adequacy till last month. Now. I had uncertainty and was questioning my instability. The emotional ground was solid a month ago and now was shaky. I was really low at this point in a room with a hundred other sick people, all waiting for lab work, all wanting good news.

My mind wandered and the séance was broken when a young girl literally collapsed on the table next to me in the large waiting room. Lying down, her head was a few feet from me, she said, "I feel so bad that I think I am going to die." A lady beside me said, "What's the matter, honey?" She said quietly, "I have had brain cancer since 1994." "I need to get to my appointment but can't walk any further."

At that point, I asked the girl, not knowing what else to say, what she needed. She said "A wheelchair to the fourth floor". She was having trouble walking. I told the lady next to me that if I was called for lab, I would be back shortly.

I found a restricted area, clearly marked "do not enter" with threats and signs. When pursuing kindness, rules are to be ignored. I rolled off a wheelchair and found myself minutes later alone with this girl, me looking down on her head, while she wept in the wheelchair. She had a husband in the military, he couldn't be here, family in Iowa, they couldn't be here either. She attended a Catholic Church in Jacksonville.

I needed to do something, but didn't know what. I got her to the appointment and signed her in. She had done chemo and radiation for the last few years. She had been told, what I had heard as an orderly 30 years ago, "Were doing all that we can do." I hated that phrase. It's so cold and passionless. So, terminal. Such a frank ending to a life. And true, hundreds of times across the country every day.

I went back to the lab room and they called my name immediately as I entered. God's time, I thought. Getting the lab work out of the way, I went to a payphone and called the Catholic Church. I encountered a secretary and told her that a Catholic, a member, I gave her the name, needed help, transportation to Mayo, and assistance in the clinic. She rolled through some list and said, "There is no record of her here." She was not cooperative but I blamed that on her age and her job title. I could have pursued above her but did not have the time. I felt the priest would certainly have assisted. I didn't blame the Catholic Church.

I then went to my next appointment on another

floor. Mayo is a list of doctors and triage to be examined by a lot of folks, residents, department heads, labs, Xray, and ultrasound, not to mention the wallet biopsy. They are extremely efficient. After one of the exams, I found the Social Services office and spoke with a social worker, advising her that a patient needed assistance. I endured a battery of questions about her name, relationship to me, how did I see her medical information and diagnosis, and the necessity of privacy issues. Red tape, as far as I was concerned.

My anger flared, I said, "This is a beautiful girl dying of a brain tumor, somebody's daughter, she has no family that can come here, she is in desperate need of social services." She seemed to relax, relented and took the name of the girl. I left.

I returned to Albany. land, in contact with others, I called the hospital social services department and told them that we would fly her family to Mayo to be with her." The lady wanted to know why. I was astounded. I said—. "Because we feel like it is the right thing to do." Social Services called a day later, said they had contacted her, and illness in her family precluded any travel. I was dejected. The final contact that I had with Mayo was a request from the hospital, a month later, for a donation to a brain tumor organization. I surmised that the patient had passed away.

After this incident, I was ashamed for my own self concern, as this girl had so much more of a problem than I ever had. When we look inward, instead of outward we become filled with self-pity and depression. I believe fully that God stuck me on that elevator that day, behind her wheelchair, looking down at the top of her head, and seemingly said, "Look at this, you self-righteous, self-absorbed, Pharisee." "Move out of your self-pity and do something for somebody less fortunate."

We may be thrown into a place where we are the only anchor that might help that person. People in this fast-paced world walk by and zone out others all around them. Ministry of any kind is not convenient. When we place ourselves in someone's life, we face all kinds of aberrant conditions. Concern cannot operate on a schedule. We must help others as the need arises. If we are cognizant, we will see the needs of others.

"For we are God's workmanship, created in Christ Jesus to do good works, which God has prepared in advance for us to do. "Ephesians 1:10

THE UNEXPLAINED

I closed my eyes tightly, the view continued. The grotesque shapes appeared. Ghoulish, frightening, blobs of blackness, monstrous images that darted and dove in the darkness. It was as if a scene was imprinted on my inner eyelids. I would tear my eyes open, and all would disappear. Life looked normal with my eyes open. The room was bright. The door was closed. The television droned on. It was an uneventful hospital stay for an acute appendicitis, done with a laparoscope three days earlier. I hoped to go home tomorrow. All was well, pain had resolved.

For the next few hours, the encounter with, whatever it was, continued. Blinking did not signal the onset. It happened only when I would close my eyes tightly for more than a few seconds, as if to rest. Swirling, thin, wisps of horrific shapes would move through the darkness. I began to wonder if I had developed some retina pathology or maybe this was a side effect of some narcotic. But I was not having pain, I had received no narcotics that day. In the next few hours, it was severe. I decided this was some mental issue, maybe a brain tumor. I hated to admit it, but the idea of demons or some spiritual evil did come to mind. I had never seen one, and didn't believe they existed. I was desperate at midnight to get some sleep. I decided, I could be losing my mind. I began to pray, nothing fervent, no promises to God that I would never stray again, I just prayed and put it to rest. I prayed as an afterthought. At that point, I was done praying and opened my eyes. I wondered what would happen if I shut them. So, I did.

I clamped my eyes shut again, waiting for all the shapes and movement of blackness to ensue. It did not. What I saw, I will never forget. With eyes closed, I saw the door to the room, the interior of the room, with the hospital door closed. There, on either side of the door way, at the top of the frame, was an angel on each corner, cherubim, reproduced exactly as you would see pictured in man's representation of what is believed from Bible descriptions. They were perched on each door post. I jerked and immediately opened my eyes, nothing was there. I immediately shut my eyes. All black. No shapes, no angels. I was shaken, but decided that I could not have seen what I thought I did. I changed my mind the next day.

The next day, the doctor spoke to me prior to discharge. He said, "You can go home but I must see you back and schedule a hemi-colectomy, surgery and another hospitalization, because you have cancer of the appendix." There are no words to describe such news. I was taken aback and stunned. I was alone, waiting on my family to take me home.

Then it dawned on me and I was shocked again. When the doctor addressed me with the news, he was standing immediately inside the doorway, between those two posts, where cherubim had perched the night before. I didn't understand it, but it gave me great comfort. I could come to no other conclusion except God was involved.

APPENDIX WHAT?

C ancer is dotted throughout all families, in young and old. Many have waited their turn for the results of the biopsy. It's not fun. When the verdict comes, there's the trauma. Someone said there was denial with diagnosis. I had read enough charts that I knew that denial would not assist me. I wanted a couple of things, peace of mind and a treatment plan. I was appalled to learn that the diagnosis of mucinous adeno- carcinoma of the appendix pivots you into a fraternity that is rare. So unusual, about one in a million. So rare, that little money is allotted at National Institute of Health for research. I found five doctors that treated it. Within a few weeks, I had received multiple opinions of treatment, mostly the same, some different.

A doctor in Washington D.C., a pioneer in the field, recommended no chemo, and surprisingly, no more surgery at present. Abdominal surgery can create scar tissue that makes later surgery for instillation of chemotherapy difficult. He didn't want to risk scar tissue filling my abdomen. He related that I may need heated intraperitoneal chemotherapy, and it would be harder with scar tissue present which is common after abdominal surgery.

A doctor at Creighton University in Omaha recommended the hemi colectomy, as had been recommended earlier. He did note that I had malignant cells on the outside of the appendix area in the pathology specimen, though margins were negative. A doctor at Wake Forest was consulted and provided excellent instruction and answered questions.

The doctor at M D Anderson in Houston, Texas was frank and recommended the hemi colectomy and avoidance of chemotherapy at present based on lack of lymph node involvement. He said, "I can give you oxaliplatin but you could have numb fingers and toes, and based on the path report, I would not take that yet." "It's a judgement call."

The Texas CT scan was more in depth than previously done. That technician said, as she injected the dye, "You will have some burning all over your body, it will light you up." She was right, no pain, but had she not issued the warning, I would have bolted from the table. A mega hot flash from toes to head as it hibernated into my midsection. I thought, "Don't let me be a GOMER, or a GONER."

I made the decision, go with the right hemi colectomy without the chemotherapy. It is best to survey the treatments, follow some recommendations and give it your best shot.

Now, for the peace part. A mortal has to resign himself to the cancer, whatever the outcome. One could say, get your affairs in order. I went on a search to meet with and find numerous people who could pray for my situation. There were many and varied prayers that went up on my behalf.

I received a call from my friend, who advised me that his congregational elders would pray with me and would anoint oil. He said, "We do what is commanded, we have no thoughts that the oil has any power, we are simply doing what God said to do." I was aware of James 5:16 that recommended this but had no knowledge of church groups having continued this past the first century. I had doubts about it. What good could become of that, either I am going to live or not. I asked a good friend to go with me, but told him that I had doubts. It was a couple of hours away and I had few nights left prior to the surgery. I needed to be home with my family. He said, "Let's go" So, we did. We traveled two hours and met in a small room in a small church. There were five in attendance that read from the bible and had prayer over me, having anointed me with oil in the process. It was a ceremony of humble, contrite men, praying and reading scripture. It was there, for the first time in my life, I realized the power of prayer. With that event, I developed a resolute attitude that I had done all I could do. I realized that there was nothing more that I could accomplish in life with the realization that it really was in God's hands now. This was the appropriate course and it was 20 years ago.

Part of my stamina that night came from growing up surrounded by prayer at home and school, something that we rarely see today in our culture. Live or die, it was now in the hands of God. I went into surgery a few days later with peace that I would have thought impossible, a young father with young children and a wife, possibly a soon to be widow. How could anything look good. Well, it didn't. But there is a realm available, that when the believer places his trust in it, there is peace that cannot be understood in natural terms.

ANGUISH

I am sick, part of my colon is missing. This was not the result of an unforeseen tragic accident, but a planned attack while I slept. The bulk of my intestines were laid upon my chest, waiting patiently, while a section was removed and dropped into a bucket. The battlefield is now covered with skin pulled so tightly that a pillow must rest against my midsection to provide some unseen relief. The only thing worse than getting up is to have someone help you up, prodding and pulling on viscera that is stretched tightly like an African tribal drum held on the rim by ten penny nails. I maneuvered and rolled slowly sideways to attain the upright position. To roll over on one side is a victory. The nurses urge you to "get up." "If you lie in bed, you will get weaker." You look helpless to the masses, so a friend asked if he could help me up. I said, "If you do, I will kill you." Perish the thought of someone pushing my body where it does not want to go. The soreness is unbelievable. Thank God, it only hurts when I move.

It literally does not hurt when I do not move. A blessing.

I lie still, like a corpse. I am unable to smile, a tube is hoisted into my nasal cavity. It travels to a large barrel beside my bed. Another leaves the bladder for the outside world. A tube is in each arm. I sense that one tube is inspiring and the other tube is expiring, life draining out. One bag holds white liquid, one holds clear liquid. I taste nothing. An ice tip on my tongue would be like a dinner on a cruise ship.

A hospital room is cold, unbending and callused. It is hard to rest and even harder to live. Cold white walls. A cold steel rod supports a television. One button gives you a crass television show and another a nurse. Your own headline is cancer. You don't care what the world has going on. Your headline has one subheading. Will I live or will I die? How long do I have? Who knows, certainly not anyone I have seen in the last 24 hours.

The surgery ~~came about~~was done in Georgia a few weeks after my consultation at M.D. Anderson in Houston, Texas. I went alone, at night, when the streets were bare, not wanting my family to be a part of this catastrophic event, the sick breadwinner. I flew from Georgia on a cheap cancer rate through Continental Airlines. Sympathy from corporate America, I liked it. The midnight cab passes a large dark building that held the recently bankrupt ENRON corporation. I thought about the people that lost all their retirement as the business collapsed. I would swap with them. Money means nothing when your health fails.

I was dropped at a sleazy motel of my own choosing, selected online. At once, I knew it was a mistake. The cheap rate that lassoed me no longer seemed appealing. I was given printed directions for turning the bathtub water on and off. I was told not to lock the bathroom door or I could become trapped. The rooms had outside doors and cats roamed the sidewalks. They rubbed on my pants legs as I walked by. The bed was inches to the floor. Meager accommodations were an understatement. The sheets were thin and parched from too many dryer spins. I decided I would be dead by mugging, cats, or rats before cancer could kill me.

I managed to get a refund and took a cab down the road. The desk clerk asked me to write a statement as to why I left or she would be fired. I was not surprised that this was a problem. On the card I wrote, "I have cancer and don't want to die here." That rattled her and she released me to the dark street corner, unimpeded, having credited me a refund.

Over the next few days, I realized, as I saw the whole health care picture at the hospital, what was happening. Where I had stayed, it was cheap, long term, housing for people receiving treatment at M D Anderson. The patients were sick and they were trying to gain health by maintaining dogs and cats, attempting to be normal in their pitiful state - trying to make a flea bag motel a home, possibly for their last days. But mostly, they wanted to live, like we all did, as we sat solemnly in the waiting areas at M D Anderson. They would be living there for months as they took chemotherapy, spending endless cab money back and forth to treatment.

As I waited for consultation in the clinics, the conversations I overheard and participated in centered around one topic, life and living. I never forgot them. One strapping muscular cowboy, who looked like perfect health, said, to his family, "All looks well but the tumors in my stomach are not smaller, they are growing.", as he patted his slim stomach. The family took it in stride. There was no silence or privacy. None was wanted. When everybody has cancer, there is some relief in the conversations ensued among complete strangers. No filters. Good support. As Tiny Tim said in The Christmas Carol, "God bless us all."

Based on the pathology report, the doctor recommended I receive a hemi colectomy. He said "I can give you oxaliplatin chemotherapy, but it could cause numb fingers and toes, and it might not recur with just the surgery." I took the surgery route with no chemotherapy. Judgement call.

I awoke last night in the dark and felt slime on my arm and down my stomach. I cut on a light and saw a bloody scene, the IV had come out and blood had drained a while on my body. It resembled a crime scene. All that was needed was yellow tape stretched around the bed perimeter. The nurse came and restarted the line as I tried to act unconcerned with the amount of blood all over my gown and dripped on the floor. I had to sit in the chair while she changed the bed. I wondered how I could be so healthy months ago and now sat with blood smeared throughout, the answer was not entirely clear.

I learned today that my lymph nodes were negative. God has given me some time, but for what? I did last longer than those in the obituaries today. How do they all die in alphabetical order?

Three or four times a day, you stagger to vertical from the supine. You are bent at a forty-five-degree angle, one foot ahead of another. The catheter hangs like a weight in gym class. The IV pole rolls along pushed by a failing body, staggering and swaying. Improvement is measured in millimeters.

I can identify with Hezekiah in Isaiah 38. He faced the wall and wept when Isaiah told him that he would not recover. I can't help but wonder if he had appendix cancer. It hits one out of a million, my lucky day. Later, God adds 15 years to his life. I like what Hezekiah compared his illness to. "I waited patiently till dawn, but like a lion, he broke all my bones, day and night you made an end to me." —"I can see that. I feel like I have been pounced upon by the king of the jungle, rolled and romped and beaten. I couldn't take offense right now at a fog rolling into the harbor. Hezekiah says he used his 15 years to tell his children about God's faithfulness. That is an inspiration.

Today the naos-gastric tube was inserted, the doctor tried to avoid it. It is similar to swallowing a garden hose covered in jelly. I remember my mother having one in her colon cancer treatment, I asked how it went to install the tube. She said, "I prayed to die." I thought that was exaggerated till I had my own. It was an accurate description. The jelly doesn't add any ease with the insertion.

I walk today to the end of the hall and back, tubes dangling and poles clanging. When I return to the bed, I will face the wall and pray like Hezekiah did.

We want order in our lives. I detected that in patients, 30 years ago in menial hospital work, white pants and all. Tragedy is unorganized. Bones splinter in all directions. Cancer metastasizes like tentacles throughout the body. A trauma, then another, then another. It strikes and turns our little part of the big world upside down. People are already walking around with unseen burdens. Their bodies are broken as well as their hearts. We crave a structure, something familiar and comforting. Wondering about our life, and the duration, is like staring at a clock that is turned upside down. There is no sense to be attained, at face value, until we look deeper, into our very soul.

I laid in the hospital bed and remembered the sudden death of my friend's father in high school. The older brother drove the younger around for hours, in the middle of the night, an attempt to calm him down, just to get him out of the house. I thought about riding in a car knowing my daddy was gone. The hum of the car did seem to give him some peace. The wheels turned but never arrived at a destination, because there wasn't one.

A passionate expression of grief or sorrow is a lament. The lament allows the Believer to see some order in the middle of tragedy. It is there in the resurrection of Jesus Christ, though it is hard to see, while sunk in the morass of sickness and grief. Jesus wept for the sorrow experienced by Mary and Martha at Lazarus' death. It's a conjugated series of events, but when Jesus was redeemed for the sin of this world, all things were promised to be made whole in eternity. Jesus conquered death and provided an exit from this world to an eternity without sickness. We strive to maintain faith and remember that, even in the hardest of times.

THE SALT OF THE EARTH

A hospital worker performed, a dull and repetitive job at 2 am every night. The unknown, white clothed orderly would come into the room and drain the urinary catheter bag, measure and clean up, job of emptying and counting a stranger's bodily fluids, excrements and vapors. He was checking intravenous fluid amounts and ~~checking the~~ integrity of the tubing. I did notice, unlike a lot of hospital staff, he did make an attempt to make less noise at the ungodly hour. That was a blessing. Some would blast the room full of light and take a blood pressure at 3 am, pumping the cuff like inflating a Michelin. A hospital is not a mecca of rest. It cannot be. On the contrary, there is no rest with the poking, prodding and pulling to obtain the accurate diagnosis. Rest is for home. Hospitals are for examinations and wide excisions.

I thought about my labors, years ago, in hospitals. It was dirty, dangerous and deadly in some cases. I did exactly what he was doing. I was glad that I did not have his job any longer. I felt smug, even in my sickened state, that I had been able to continue education in healthcare and seemingly advance myself.

From the darkness one night, as the man poured and measured, he said, "We are praying for you in Sunday School class.—" I said. "You are?" He said, "Yes." And called me by name. I gulped as he left the room. Here was a menial worker, who did not know me personally, but was the salt of the earth. He was a believer who took his belief seriously and prayed. His low position was used as a blessing to God. It was not a stepping stone to an advanced position in hierarchy. His advancement was eternal, holy and was in the Kingdom, not the world. His timecard was punched by God and not the time clock. The job was a glory to God and a blessing to people like me. I pondered.

Strangely, I never saw the worker again. He came into my world with his cups and bottles, but I knew this was a God thing- some arrangement to shake me back again to my senses, and learn the true value of people. Sometimes, God seizes hearts and pivots us toward the right path. The depths of despair and uncertainty can be the beginning of a pure and grateful heart.

My full pathology report is back. The specimen has been reviewed and sliced open like a tomato. A man in a crisp, white coat and thick rubber gloves has dissected all parts removed from my body. He was given two feet of right colon and asked to determine the cellular makeup.

I hope the proper name identification has been done. It would be a shame to give a fellow from Des Moines my diagnosis. That, of course, has been done before. Mislabeled bits and pieces of the human body, names misspelled, smeared ink, can all result in a host of misinformation and false conclusions.

The pathologist has rendered his opinion on my body parts and the insurance company has been billed. He is about to turn my universe upside down, ~~but~~ he doesn't have to even see me or know me. He knows me as a glass slide that holds malignant cells. The doctor that split me open will announce the news.

All of a sudden, the focus is blurry. Everything that was important is no longer important now. Images have switched places. We stand on jelly in the middle of a big world. What was solid is now sinking sand.

We could imitate part of Jonah's life and have our friends throw us off the boat. Run away from God, wind up in the belly of a big fish for a few days and come out on dry land. Sounds intriguing. But,

God doesn't cause misery, God is good. The world has misery. But God can use a misery to change us-to improve our relationship with him. We are in a broken state. With God's help we can make sense of the pieces. We are told to rejoice, not from the state we are in, but for the God of the Bible who is beside us and with us, each step.

THE SPIT COLLECTOR

We are unaware of our body functions unless our body doesn't function anymore. Sights and sounds of a healing body, none make for pleasant conversation. I became aware of having extreme salivation. Spit would fill my mouth like some stream from somewhere in my body. I would have to either swallow or spit it out. One of two actions was required. I would drift into a blurry realm of unconsciousness awakening only to swallow again. This was repeated over one night for a period of hours. It was leaking out the sides of my mouth when I woke up.

Like an engineer mapping out a company solution, I decided it had started with some intravenous dose of something. I had to have relief. I searched for a solution. My head would wedge sideways between the railing and the pillow. An emesis basin would fit 7 inches from the salivating orifice crammed into this space at the rail. I could flow into the basin, unimpeded. This was a minor miracle to me, not having to wake up and swallow. There was rest for the weary. I was grateful.

I laid there in my semi- awake stupor pondering my invention. Maybe it could be patented. A sponge would be installed into the bottom for rapid absorption. And on and on. Probably more useless things have been invented in this world. My problem had dissipated by morning and the solution was swiftly forgotten.

Paul makes an observation in 2 Corinthians 4:7. We are clay pots, meaning we are imperfect, mortal vessels that can lead us to the notion that God is the one in control. The faulty, cancer ridden, imperfect, warranty free pot, cannot maintain anything without God. When the diagnosis comes, we realize just how little we are in control. Stephen, the deacon, preached a sermon, then he died. He died and his clay pot was crushed with stones from the mad crowd. Before death, he saw Jesus standing beside the throne of God. Jesus stood up for Stephen. We can't understand why Stephen couldn't live. He never had appendix cancer. He never had uncontrollable spit. He never had to pray for a relief from cancer. But he was murdered. Would not it have been better had he lived and stayed in the world?

God's ways are not man's ways. The world cannot destroy the Christian. We are eternal. We complain like the Israelites and wish that we had never left Egypt. Paul said in 2 Corinthians that we are wasting away in the body, but are achieving an eternal glory that outweighs the world. Jesus stands for us and we reach for him. That is the only solution.

HONORABLE SUPREME COURT JUSTICE CLARENCE THOMAS

In October, 1991, Columbus, Georgia, the seven-year-old child walked through the living room, glanced at the television, and observed a well-dressed man sitting at a table, perspiring under bright lights. He was being questioned by a group in front of him. The child paused, studied the screen, and listened. Questions were being asked to the man. She pointed and said, "Why are they being mean to that man?" I was surprised at her indication that she picked up on a contentious situation, the confirmation hearings in Washington, D.C. of Honorable Justice Clarence Thomas. Young children have ability to analyze any verbal response as to its importance or the emotion that may lie in it. She had picked this up in seconds.

As our generation was raised with respect to government and leaders, I responded and said," Why don't you send him a letter?" She sat down and wrote in block print, a letter of a few sentences of how she felt. My wife and I attached a cover letter and mailed it to his office. We felt we had shown our daughter how it works in government and political matters. We certainly never expected an acknowledgement. Seven months later, to our surprise, she received a letter from Justice Thomas inviting us to the Supreme Court. I called the secretary and asked her to pick the date at his convenience. The visit was scheduled a year later.

We visited Washington D.C. prior to the visit. In the touring, the youngest daughter lacerated her head skipping and falling on the Lincoln Monument. A bumpy ambulance ride, with her strapped to a board transpired with her yelling, "I'm not wearing this to school." Upon hearing the child crying, the nurse at George Washington Trauma Center told us to calm down, that she had taken care of President Reagan when he was shot and our daughter would do fine. I jerked as I thought of that bit of history that the nurse was a part of. Our daughter did well and wore her head bandaged to the Supreme Court.

Justice Thomas was a congenial, kind, warm man and talked with us about the Supreme Court for a couple of hours. He has a great sense of humor and my four-year-old said, "you have a laugh like Santa Claus." He grew up outside Savannah, Georgia in an enclave called Pinpoint. His family was a major influence on his life and his grandfather made sure he was educated. As we all did, he grew up in a culture of God in society and schools. There was deep spiritual influence from his family, especially his grandfather. Initially, desiring to be a priest, Justice Thomas attended two years of seminary in Savannah, Georgia at St John Vianney Minor Seminary. An Albany resident that we knew had also attended during those years.

Justice Thomas grew up impoverished, and developed a work ethic as well as a strong faith in God. We toured the Supreme Court chambers and my daughter was allowed to sit in his chair behind the bar. It was truly memorable and impressed upon us the rule of law, at the highest court in the land.

Justice Thomas said, "When you leave, after experiencing this, you will turn back, look at the structure and say, "Truly, this is the Supreme Court." He was exactly right. When we saw the numerous historical paintings, the décor, and the magnificence, several of the Justices and the surroundings, we knew that this truly was the highest legal authority in our land.

We yearned to observe the proceedings and years later, we were allowed to return and sit in the courtroom listening to arguments. We saw one of the last appearances of Justice Rehnquist and the other justices, some now retired. We watched Attorney Ted Olson, the Solicitor General, who lost his wife in the Pentagon plane crash, argue a case. It gives a person a new respect for the law and love for our system of government and the people who work tirelessly within it.

THE ENDING

The minister lies under crisp, white sheets, nonresponsive, with the rhythmic sounds of a ventilator filling the room. He has been in this condition for two months. Brain activity is ending. There will be no more sermons in this life. The pulpit has been entered for the last time. With family consent, nurses turn the machine off and dying begins. It takes about two hours. The heart eventually stops contracting, it knows this is a terminal job. The heart monitor line goes flat. No alarms sound. It is not a code, where frantic doctors will administer lifesaving epinephrine and shock paddles in an effort to keep the patient alive. A granddaughter, informs his son, in a waiting room. The moment is here. Its time.

As the son went up the stairs, he thought of the death of his mother ten years earlier, at age 61. He had left her at the hospital, at midnight, with father and brother asleep adjacent to the bed. When he crawled into bed at home, a voice spoke, "Go back to the hospital." He left the bed that he had just entered, as his wife said, "Where are you going?" He said, "Did you hear anything?" "No." She remarked. He dressed and returned to the hospital room where his brother and father were asleep. He went to his mother's side and stared down as he raised an eyelid. The pupil constricted as it would in a living person. In a few seconds, the pupil dilated and fixed. She had passed from life with the family in the room.

Arriving at the bedside of his father, he studies the monitor with the line trailing flat on the screen. The father is gone. The son leans down and says, "We love you, and will see you on those streets of gold in heaven." The monitor, when the sentence is finished, leaps into normal sinus rhythm with the QRS complex traveling across the screen for 30 more seconds. Then, it flatlines a second time. It is not erratic heart activity. It is the last earthly goodbye from a father to a son.

Like other strange occurrences in the families, this is attributed to spirituality, angels or the Holy Spirit. The Bible says that believers have it, angels are called "ministering spirits", and the Holy Spirit "intercedes". How much plainer does it have to be? Three residents standing against the wall are staring at the monitor intently. They say nothing but there are questions expressed by their countenance.

So, this is the end of a story about the effects and layers of influence that the fire and brimstone sermon, as well as the culture of God in the classroom and on society, had on America and on a generation. Are we indeed hanging by a thread that is on fire, as Jonathan Edwards preached in 1741? Or, am Am I held in the hand of God, protected from all those demons at the gates of hell? Was the noise of the pulpit loud but the screams of the children still drowned out the message? Did we humanly ignore it and ridicule the loud preacher for saying it?

The nature of God is not altered by a type of sermon, the intonation of a minister's voice, or a bad actor in the pulpit. The nature of God that moved on the waters with Jesus and the Holy Spirit at the creation of the world is not changed by a method of preaching style. The nature of God is seen in his autobiography, the Bible, written over a period of 1500 years, by men led by the Holy Spirit. They describe creation, salvation, heaven, a story of redemption and the coming judgement.

Scrawled on the wall of a filthy, smelly, condemned, bathroom, uneven, and with a scratchy old black marker, was, "Jesus is Lord" and underneath, "Repent for the Kingdom of Heaven is at Hand." An eight-year-old grandchild remarked, "That's a believer." It was the farthest thing from my mind, which was occupied with finding the nearest exit. The bathroom would have won the award for filthiest between South Georgia and Atlanta.

Over the next few days, I realized that when children point out the obvious, we overlook that Jesus said, "You must become as little children." We must think like them. It is not easy for adults to do that, due to a myriad of problems, preconceived behaviors and our own biased worldly opinions.

Polycarp, a church bishop in 155 A D, was burned at the stake for refusing to say "Caesar is Lord." Instead, he said, "Jesus is Lord." John the Baptist said "Repent for the Kingdom of Heaven is at hand." It cost him his life, as Herod Antipas, the political leader, demanded his death. Jesus was crucified by political and religious leaders for the same plea. Certainly, the world would be absolved and a better place, if we heeded the comments by a child and returned to a message penned on a dirty bathroom wall.

MY LITTLE MEPHIBOSHETH

An epic story of kindness in the Bible is the action King David took dealing with the disabled son of Jonathan, grandson of Saul, the mortal enemy of David. Both Jonathan and Saul had died in battle. David asked the amazing question, "Is there anyone of the House of Saul that I can show kindness? " Mephibosheth then lived out his days in David's royal palace at the king's table. This provides such a wonderful example for the families of disabled children everywhere, the tender concern and Providence that God has for his children.

Wells Middleton Grant is a beautiful grandchild with Joubert's Syndrome, a rare genetic disorder. He is now 18 months old and in physical therapy and many other medical endeavors due to absence of a portion of his cerebellum. He never stops smiling and seems to be surrounded with God's presence. He smiles so boldly and has sparkling eyes that even when crying seem angelic. This has provided great solace for the family, that even as Wells may not be aware of the swirling of prayers around him, his future is comfortable in the Hand of God, as all disabled children are. Children occupied a special place in the heart of Jesus, as he ministered on earth. He welcomed children when the adults pushed them aside, and said, "You must become as little children."

The story of the Bible begins with "God created the heavens and the earth." and ends with a "new heaven and a new earth." (Rev 21:1) Little Wells and others will be made whole. There will be no tears, sickness or death. All infirmities and inequalities will be made new. Loved ones will be seen and known and united with their children. Grief will no longer be a word. The fallen world will be made new. Evil will disappear. Jesus will reign supreme. Believers have a hope that is beyond comprehension because of what Jesus did on the Cross, dying for the sins of the world.

One minister said it so well. "If the name of God is linked with someone, they are going to be all right." Satan cannot break that link. That is the link that Wells and his family have, he is going to be all right.

ACKNOWLEDGEMENT

Stories preserved from the past are relevant to the future and are an inspiration, as we walk along the same road of life that our ancestors took. In recounting, we remember those who went before us and their sacrifices, hardships and manner of overcoming obstacles. We are all living stories, and all of us have something to share and a story "worth telling."

Appreciation to the Colquitt/Miller Arts Council (CMAC) and its project, Swamp Gravy, for promoting the telling and recording of stories in order to keep story telling alive and on the stage of community theater, for the world to see.

ABOUT THE AUTHOR

Dr. Ted Ary grew up in Moultrie, Georgia, attended Harding University, Illinois College of Podiatric Medicine and a hospital program at Doctor's Hospital, Tucker, Georgia. He practiced Podiatric Medicine and Surgery for 40 years in South Georgia before retiring. He enjoys his family of 4 daughters, 12 grandchildren and two dogs. He loves writing, enjoys the beach and the mountains, spending time in both. He chose to write this book so his children and grandchildren could see a slice of life from the vantage point of their forefathers.

Made in the USA
Middletown, DE
28 February 2023

25611407R00159